צדקה
Tzedakah:
A Time For Change

DANNY SIEGEL

Edited by Karen L. Stein

United Synagogue of Conservative Judaism — Department of Youth Activities

UNITED SYNAGOGUE OF CONSERVATIVE JUDAISM

DEPARTMENT OF YOUTH ACTIVITIES

Jules A. Gutin	DIRECTOR
Karen L. Stein	ASSISTANT DIRECTOR
Aviva Tilles	PROJECTS DIRECTOR
Ilan Schwartz	PROGRAM COORDINATOR
Shira Steinberg	CHAPTER SERVICES COORDINATOR
Adam Kofinas	MEETINGS MANAGER
Matthew Halpern	COMMUNICATIONS COORDINATOR
Nahum Binder	CENTRAL SHALIACH
David Keren	DIRECTOR, ISRAEL PROGRAMS
Yitzchak Jacobsen	DIRECTOR, ISRAEL OFFICE
Yossi Garr	DIRECTOR, NATIV

INTERNATIONAL YOUTH COMMISSION

Paul Kochberg, CHAIRPERSON

UNITED SYNAGOGUE OF CONSERVATIVE JUDAISM

Dr. Ray Goldstein, INTERNATIONAL PRESIDENT
Rabbi Jerome M. Epstein, EXECUTIVE VICE-PRESIDENT
Dr. Marilyn Lishnoff Wind, VICE PRESIDENT FOR YOUTH SERVICES AND EDUCATION

A publication of the International Youth Commission
United Synagogue of Conservative Judaism
155 Fifth Avenue, New York, New York 10010
http://www.uscj.org/usy

First Edition, 2007
Copyright 2007 United Synagogue Youth

Printed and bound in the United States of America by Howard Press
Cover design by Matthew Halpern
Production, layout and design by Karen L. Stein, Project Editor

Contents

Editor's Note

Many of us are uncomfortable speaking about money. We don't like to ask to borrow, and we don't like to lend. It's not polite to ask someone how much money she makes, or to question someone on how much is in his bank account. We pass people on the street asking for money and are not sure what to do, so we turn away. We aren't sure which solicitations are "legit" so we toss aside envelopes and emails. We are great at collecting cans of food, used clothing, or other needed items, but can't always get them into the hands that need them. Simply put, we are lost when it comes to reaching into our pockets and changing the world.

Tzedakah: A Time to Change is more than a theoretical discussion about Tzedakah. It is designed to teach us how to better utilize our Tzedakah funds and how to begin discussions about money in a realistic and productive way. We will grapple with the challenges of collecting and distributing Tzedakah, and learn to make wise decisions about our own allocations and personal spending. We are very fortunate that reknowned Tzedakah educator, poet and author, Danny Siegel, has brought this topic to life. A talented educator and scholar, Danny has enabled classical Jewish sources to speak to modern considerations about Tzedakah. It has been a privilege to work with him throughout the transformation of this book and to ignite the true power of Tzedakah.

This sourcebook is based largely on the book *Giving Your Money Away: How Much, How To, Why, When, and to Whom: Danny Siegel's Practical Guide to Personalized Tzedakah* (Town House Press, 2006). Danny played a very strong role in the adaptation and development of this sourcebook. We are grateful to Danny for always being available to brainstorm or help find additional resources that would help shape the interactive educational components of this sourcebook.

It is with great appreciation that we acknowledge the readers whose talents and suggestions helped to improve this sourcebook: Merrill Alpert, Arnie Draiman, Rabbi Paul Drazen, Rabbi Jerome M. Epstein, Jonathan S. Greenberg, Jules A. Gutin, Joshua Rabin, Michelle Rich, Amee Huppin Sherer and David Srebnick. In addition, we are grateful to Arthur Kurzweil for enthusiastically granting permission to reprint his important article about beggars.

I am grateful to my colleagues in the Youth Department of the United Synagogue of Conservative Judaism who have all been extremely encouraging throughout the entire process of work on this sourcebook. Additionally, I am most grateful to my husband, Adam Monaco, who is always there to support me and understands that the "Mitzvahs" we do each day in our line of work sometimes takes long hours, and a lot of patience.

Karen L. Stein
November, 2007

צדקה–*Tzedakah: A Time For Change*

Preface

I can still remember a study session I attended at a regional USY convention in Atlantic City, New Jersey. It was back in the 1960's at the old Breakers Hotel (of blessed memory.) The teacher inspired us. He was a little off-beat, but maybe that was one of the reasons why we soaked up every word. Over forty years later, I continue to learn important lessons from that teacher, and I'm sure you will, as well, when you read through the pages of this book.

Not too many years after that first encounter, I was a member of the Central USY staff. One of my responsibilities was the coordination of the USY Israel Pilgrimage educational program. I was sitting in another one of Danny Siegel's sessions. This one was at the annual convention of the Jewish Youth Directors' Association. I think it was in 1976. Danny gave an inspiring talk about Tzedakah with a treasure trove of practical ideas as to how we could translate our studies into action in our communities and in our daily lives. I was sitting with a colleague, Sandy Silverstein, who handled much of the administration of the USY Israel Pilgrimage program. We realized that the same lessons Danny was teaching us at a hotel in the Catskills in New York State, could be taught to hundreds of USYers on our Israel Pilgrimage program. Not long after the conference, we began to work out the details. And so began a journey which is still in progress.

Over thirty years later the children of those USYers who were inspired by Danny can now be found walking through the streets of Jerusalem, meeting his "Mitzvah Heroes" and learning about the deeper meaning of Tzedakah.

Those USYers on the 1976 Israel Pilgrimage went back to their communities and began to change the world. All of a sudden we began to ask deeper questions during our Tikun Olam Tzedakah Fund Allocations process. Just a few years later the USYers decided that their regional conventions and the International Convention had to include Tzedakah and community service projects. We even created a special USY on Wheels bus, Mission: Mitzvah, which devotes even more time to helping others.

I have no doubt that many thousands of lives have been touched because of an inspirational moment in 1976 I'm not just talking about the thousands of USYers who have been inspired by Danny since that summer. I'm talking about the lives which were improved from hundreds of thousands of Tzedakah dollars, tons of donated food, truck loads of clothing, boxes of toiletries, cases of canned goods, thousands of volunteers, hundreds of "Mitzvah Clowns"... The list is endless!

Who says one person can't make a difference? We know otherwise. That's one of the most important lessons I have learned from Danny. I have no doubt you will learn that, and much, much more as you read through the pages of this book.

May we all be inspired by these valuable lessons and merit to continue to make the world a better place.

Jules A. Gutin
International USY Director
New York, November, 2007

Introduction

by Danny Siegel

I. Today's USYers As Quality Tikun Olamniks

The sheer quantity and range of USY'ers Tikun Olam Mitzvahs is truly staggering. The experience they have and the experiences they describe in telling their stories orally and in print cover everything from acts of Gemillut Chassadim with Elders, with people living in precarious economic conditions, with individuals and groups with various disabilities, with disaster relief programs, global and local issues - in apparently every area of need conceivable, USY'ers have been active, pro-active, and effective in astonishingly impressive fashion.

I have been most fortunate to follow their activities and to be a part of some of these Grand Acts of Caring, Lovingkindness for many years. Since 1976, I have served as USY Pilgrimage Tzedakah Resource Person, which has allowed me to observe and join more than 15,000 of these marvelous teen-agers as they (a) experienced encounters with Giants of Tikun Olam (whom I call Mitzvah heroes), and (b) frequently performing their hands-on Mitzvah magic with a huge array of Mitzvah heroes and Tzedakah organizations in Israel. At day's end, I am often exhausted - not so much from the physical energy expended while working with them. It is rather the emotional and spiritual uplift of watching them at their Tikun Olam work and listening to them during the give-and-take of my talks and during informal schmooze time with them throughout the day...this, besides the hundreds of encounters I have had with them when I am "on the road" speaking at their local synagogues, regional conventions, or encampments.

I can summarize this phenomenon very simply: By now it is a Very Big Duh! for me to ask a group, "How many of you have ever worked with children or adults with disabilities?" Hands shoot up. (Duh!) "With Elders in nursing homes or in their own homes?" Hands, more hands. (Duh!) "Served in a soup kitchen?" "Conducted a food drive?" "Collected old cellphones and donated them to women who are victims of domestic violence?" Still more hands up and USY'ers eager to share their stories with me. (Duh!)

II. Money Mitzvahs
      1. Since Jewish tradition clearly teaches that Tikun Olam involves two Mitzvahs -
          A. Tzedakah (money) and
          B. Gemillut Chassadim (time, effort, energy, physical activity),
      2. And since USY'ers have demonstrated incredibly fine experience in the area of Tikun Olam,
      3. USY decided this year to devote its sourcebook and convention study essentially to in-depth study of Tzedakah money
          A. What our Jewish sources teach us about the unique Jewish way of giving and
          B. How to distribute Tzedakah money wisely.

Of course, USY'ers have had extensive experience with Tzedakah money through the Social Action-Tikun Olam (SATO) Program. The purpose of this sourcebook, then, is meant to extend both their overall understanding of Tzedakah in their lives and their practical knowledge of evaluating where, when, and how much to give.

This sourcebook is almost exclusively based on my book *Giving Your Money Away - How Much, How to, Why, When, and to Whom: Danny Siegel's Practical Guide to Personalized Tzedakah* (Town House Press, 2006). Significant adaptations and supplementary material have shaped it specifically as a sourcebook, and it is hoped that this material will help refine the USY'ers abilities to make many more Tikun Olam miracles happen through their Mitzvah-money efforts - not only during their time in USY, but long into the future. For myself, gathering the material for my book and actually writing it sharpened my abilities in more areas of Tzedakah than I would have imagined when I began the process.

III. Todah and Yasher Koach!
I would like to thank Jules Gutin, USY's Director and my personal friend of many years for approaching me at last year's convention about the possibility of using my material as a basis for this sourcebook.

I wish to thank Karen Stein who adapted my material and who gently worked with me - authors can be very touchy about their writings - to shape a book into a sourcebook.

In addition, there were several other readers who offered suggestions, two of whom I would like to single out for my thanks: Arnie Draiman, former Pilgrimage group leader for several years (among other USY positions), and Amee Huppin Sherer, former Pinwheel President. Both added important insights to the finished product.

Yishar Kochachem to all who participated in the process, and

To all who will use the material for the sake of Tikun Olam, לחיים-Lechaim - to Life! Tzedakah is an awesome force-for-Life which allows every one of us to work wonders on behalf of others.

P.S. Two editorial notes:

(1) I always use words such as "Tzedakah" in my writings. I believe that capitalization gives added emphasis to the all-imporant concept and reality I am discussing.

(2) When I am writing or speaking about Tzedakah, Gemillut Chassadim, and Tikun Olam, I always use the word "Mitzvahs" (and not "Mitzvot") as the plural form. I most assuredly recognize the double meaning of "Mitzvah" as both "commandment" and "doing something good". Nevertheless, when someone hears a phrase like "He's/she's doing lots of Mitzvahs", the connotation is "doing good things for people."

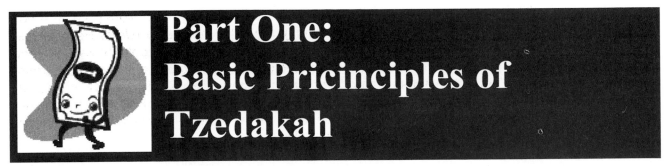

Part One: Basic Pricinciples of Tzedakah

Defining Terms

There are a few essential terms you need to know to do your Tzedakah Jewishly: מצוה-Mitzvah, צדקה-Tzedakah, גמילות חסדים-Gemillut Chassadim, תיקון עולם-Tikun Olam, and כבוד-Kavod.

מצוה—**Mitzvah** has two essential meanings: "commandment" and "good deed." Except as otherwise specified, in this book, we will refer to the latter definition.

צדקה—**Tzedakah**, from the Hebrew root צ-ד-ק means "justice, doing the right thing", and is used primarily in this book to refer to using your money for the benefit of others. This term will be explained in greater detail throughout this sourcebook. I also refer to a "צדיק-Tzaddik (m)/ צדקת-Tzadeket (f)", meaning "Good Person, a man/woman who does Tzedakah".

גמילות חסדים—**Gemillut Chassadim** refers to physical acts of caring lovingkindness, i.e., using your time, talents, energy, and efforts (volunteering) for תיקון עולם—**Tikun Olam**, fixing the world in any and every way possible. Clearly, both Tzedakah and Gemillut Chassadim are crucial elements for making complete Tikun Olam happen. However, my focus in this sourcebook is on the part the enormous power money has to change the world. In no way do I wish to imply that your time, energy, and effort are of secondary importance. A thorough study of Gemillut Chassadim may be found in my book *Who, Me? Yes, You! — Danny Siegel's Workbook to Help You Decide Where, When, Why, and How You Can Do Your Best Tikkun Olam.*

כבוד—**Kavod** means "dignity", "self-dignity", "human dignity", a vital element in all acts of Tzedakah. There is always a need to preserve not only the dignity of the recipient, but also of the giver. The issue of Kavod extends even to our use of other words and phrases. For example, using terms such as "the poor" or "the disabled" has an element of depersonalization. Individuals become categories of people. Phrases such as "individuals in need" and "persons with disabilities" would be the preferred terms. Similarly, "politically correct" vocabulary is an attempt to provide the most sensitive terms for various types or classes of human beings.

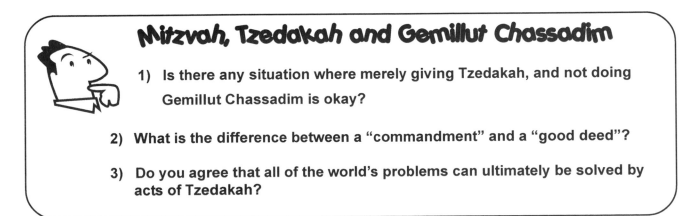

Mitzvah, Tzedakah and Gemillut Chassadim

1) Is there any situation where merely giving Tzedakah, and not doing Gemillut Chassadim is okay?

2) What is the difference between a "commandment" and a "good deed"?

3) Do you agree that all of the world's problems can ultimately be solved by acts of Tzedakah?

Let's look at three additional terms — Tzedakah, charity and philanthropy. While all three terms refer to providing for others, by examining the origins of the words, you will recognize that there are significant differences. It is true that there are areas that overlap. However, the unique practice of "Tzedakah" becomes evident when you examine where their meanings diverge.

"**Charity**" comes from the word "caritas", the Latin word for "love".

"**Philanthropy**" is composed of two Greek elements: the "phil" part means "love", and the "anthropy" (from "anthropos") means "man", "love of man". (In the 21st century, we would say, "love of humanity".)

"**Tzedakah**" (and its intimately-related term "Tzedek") comes from the ancient Hebrew root "צדק", meaning "justice", "the right thing to do". As I see it, one advantage of the term "Tzedakah" is that, if it is your starting point for giving, it is extremely easy to find things that are wrong in the world which you can make right by doing Tzedakah. In fact, you may not be a particularly "loving person", but you can still do Tzedakah. Or you may find a situation where someone you don't love or don't even like is in need, and you will still do something for that person's benefit.

In addition, in several passages in Biblical literature "Tzedek" and "Tzedakah" mean "victory". The implication is clear: The good and the right ultimately win out in the world and in Life. In the broadest, almost cosmic sense, these terms mean that all the world's problems are ultimately solvable by acts of Tzedakah. As my teacher, Rabbi Arthur Green has translated the words of the famous Chassidic Rebbi, Rabbi Nachman of Bratzlav, "Despair is not an option-אין שום יאוש בעולם כלל".

And, furthermore, according to some Biblical philologists, "Tzedek" and "Tzedakah" can also be translated as "success". This is surely a most powerful re-definition for anyone who is looking to be "successful" in life.

Thinking It Through
Tzedakah, Philanthopy and Charity

Defining Terms: Define the following words using your own words to differentiate one from the other:

Tzedakah:

Charity:

Philanthropy:

Gemillut Chassadim:

Tikun Olam:

Mitzvah:

Meet the Mitzvah Heroes

As you read this guide, I write about trust and reliability as the most important issues to consider when deciding where to contribute your Tzedakah money. Since Mitzvah heroes personify trustworthiness and reliability, it is important to explain what I mean by the term "Mitzvah hero". The following is based on my experience of more than three decades working with more than 200 of these remarkable human beings.

Mitzvah heroes are giants of Tikun Olam. They are experts in this field because they are intensely involved in changing lives by small, medium, and large Mitzvah-deeds. It is because of their Tikun Olam work that they have a profound understanding of the essence of caring, power-as-Mitzvah-power, and the nature of people as human beings. Many seem to have been born with a deep sensitivity to the needs of others and to respond by their actions directly and powerfully to those needs. Others developed and refined their latent Tikun Olam sensibilities and skills as they continued their holy work.

Mitzvah heroes are men and women of all ages, intelligence, educational background, religious affiliation, and economic status. Some see themselves as destined from birth for this kind of Grand Endeavor, and others still express surprise at themselves for having taken this path in life. All of them are inspired and inspiring and delightful to be with, individuals of the highest personal integrity, absolutely trustworthy, and all of them have one concern and one concern alone: that the lives of other people should and can be made better by their actions.

People who meet them are universally struck by how authentic they are. Mitzvah heroes are the best-of-the-best human beings they have ever met. For these reasons alone, your list of potentially worthy recipients of your Tzedakah money should consider Mitzvah heroes and their Tikun Olam work. But, there are additional reasons to consider Mitzvah heroes. None of them is comfortable with the label, "Mitzvah hero", but they are willing to be known as teachers. They are, indeed, the best teachers of Mitzvahs, Tzedakah, and Tikun Olam. If it is the very nature of "Mitzvah hero-ness" to be Tikun Olam teachers, then we ought to learn about them and their work, meet them, spend our time with them, work with them, and, as a consequence of so doing, learn from them…and most definitely support them with our Tzedakah money. To analogize: When looking for the right graduate school, a student looks for two things — the right kind of program and certain specific professors who are the best in their field. A master's in drama, might lead you to two choices — a program that stresses academics, or one that teaches everything about hands-on acting, playwriting, and the art and mechanics of stage design and lighting. Having chosen which kind of drama program is best, the student then has to pick the program where the right professor for his or her own specific needs is teaching. Certainly, then, if the field of endeavor is Fixing the World, What Makes Good People Good, Life Itself, and the Meaning of Life, the wise decision would be for you to meet Mitzvah heroes, and to learn to do Tikun Olam the way they do it. You, then, carry those lessons further and do your own kind of Tikun Olam.

For some people (myself included), Mitzvah heroes may even have the answer to the question, "What is the meaning of life?". Their answer: Life is Mitzvahs. The Mitzvah hero might state it in different words, such as, "Some people first want to understand all of the 'Why of It All' and then to act. It is really the other way around. First of all, you do: You hold the hand of the lonely person; you spoon-feed an Elder who can no longer feed herself or himself, you pay a scholarship at a swimming pool or for therapeutic horseback riding lessons for someone damaged by a stroke so he or she can have a better chance at 100% rehabilita-

> When The Good Person is in a community, that person is its radiance, its glory, and its brilliance.
> (Midrash Ruth Rabbah 2:12)

tion. You do those things, and after you have done them, then you will have a better understanding of the 'Why of It All'. If you ask and ask and spend years asking, you may have missed out." This is just one of the many lessons to be absorbed when working with and supporting Mitzvah heroes.

Throughout this book, I refer to several of my own Mitzvah heroes. You will become familiar with names like Anita Shkedi, PK Beville, Dr. William Thomas, Ray Buchanan, Joseph Gitler, Kathy Freund, and Avshalom Beni. Their work — as well as that of 100 of my other Mitzvah heroes — is described in the "Annual Reports" section of my Ziv Tzedakah Fund website, www.ziv.org. You, yourself, most likely already know some Mitzvah heroes, and will discover others through your own research and Tikun Olam work. The end result will most certainly be a more refined, efficient, extensive, and meaningful use of your Tzedakah money.

 Thinking It Through

1. How would you **find** Mitzvah heroes?

2. How much would you go out of your way to **meet** Mitzvah heroes?

3. What would you want **to do** with them?

4. What would you **want** to learn from them?

5. What would you **expect** to learn from them?

6. What would you **hope** to learn from them?

The Pedestal

Mitzvah Heroes. Just plain everyday people who made big-time Tikun Olam happen. The good thing to do is to meet them, watch them at their Mitzvah work, listen to them, and learn from them. Draw close to them, not as a fawning, unquestioning disciple, but rather as one who shares their vision. The not-so-good thing to do is to put them on a pedestal and admire them and stand in awe of them. It separates us from them, keeps us at a safe, but unfortunate, distance. Though I have used the educator John Holt's quote in a number of my books, I use it again here, because it is so apropos:

*"Charismatic leaders make us think,
'Oh, if only I could do that, be like that.'
True leaders make us think, 'If they can do that, then...I can too.'"*

Mitzvah heroes *are* awesome because their Mitzvah work is awesome. For example, Kathy Freund, concerned about the dangers of some Elders who were no longer able to drive safely, established the Independent Travel Network (ITN) in Portland, Maine. It provides (mostly) volunteer drivers to transport Elders to the market, doctor, hairdresser, wherever they need to go, all for a very nominal fee. It is a *very* impressive program and it benefits so many Elders, particularly those who are unable to use public transportation, afford cabs, or don't have relatives or friends to drive them.

If we stand back and merely admire Ms. Freund and others like her, we miss the point. "If they can do that, then...[to whatever extent I, myself, am able], I can, too." *They* don't want to be on a pedestal, so don't feel a need to put them there. There is no need to be afraid that this will blow our egos out of proportion. This is not about ego; it is about Tikun Olam, and, if anything, that makes for quite an opposite reaction, i.e., a very humbling feeling to be a part of this Grand and Holy Work. In November, 1999, Ziv Tzedakah Fund sponsored its first "Mitzvah Heroes Conference". Gathered together were 90 people, 15 of whom were the very personalities whose stories I have been recounting for years. All of this packed into a day-and-a-half. It was *extremely* intense. But the participants knew we were there together to see what we had in common with the teachers, and then to apply our own talents and time and energy to do as they do.

No pedestals!

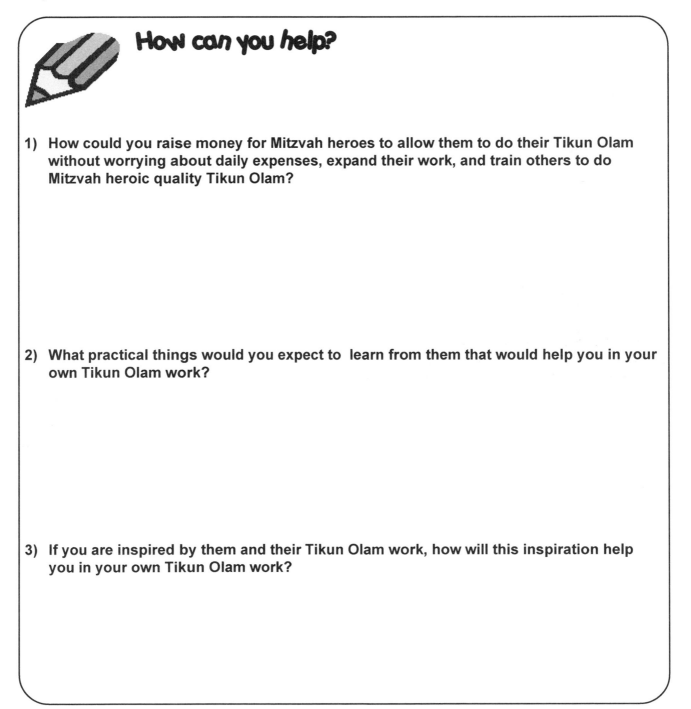

How can you help?

1) How could you raise money for Mitzvah heroes to allow them to do their Tikun Olam without worrying about daily expenses, expand their work, and train others to do Mitzvah heroic quality Tikun Olam?

2) What practical things would you expect to learn from them that would help you in your own Tikun Olam work?

3) If you are inspired by them and their Tikun Olam work, how will this inspiration help you in your own Tikun Olam work?

Why Give?

הִנֵּה תָּאַבְתִּי לְפִקֻּדֶיךָ בְּצִדְקָתְךָ חַיֵּנִי

I love your Mitzvahs.
Give me Life through Your Tzedakah.

(Psalm 119:40)

Life is a short-term interest-bearing loan. Tikun Olam is the interest you pay.
(Professor Eliezer Jaffe, Tzedakah Rebbi to the author and founder of the Israel Free Loan Association.)

Many of our classic texts teach that a Jew should do Mitzvahs because they are just that — Mitzvahs. They are God's commandments, guiding us through this precious gift called "Life" and filling our days, hours, and moments with meaning. In some sense, they are intended to show us how our years, days, hours, and even our moments may best be appreciated and put to holy use. One of the first instructions God gives to Abraham is:

Mitzvah commanded in Torah:

כִּי יְדַעְתִּיו לְמַעַן אֲשֶׁר יְצַוֶּה אֶת־בָּנָיו וְאֶת־בֵּיתוֹ
אַחֲרָיו וְשָׁמְרוּ דֶּרֶךְ יְהֹוָה לַעֲשׂוֹת צְדָקָה וּמִשְׁפָּט

"For I have selected him [Abraham] so that he may instruct his children and his posterity after him to keep God's ways: to do what is just and right [Tzedakah U'Mishpat]"

(Bereishit 18:19)

> **What do you think this means? How can one be commanded to do what is just and right?**

Furthermore, Jewish tradition takes the position that our deeds form our thoughts, and not the other way around. It is by doing that we form our attitudes; the way we act has the power to bring us to an intellectual and spiritual appreciation for the sanctity of Life. Finally, our tradition demonstrates a deep understanding of human motivations. Human beings — because they are human — are not always capable of behavior inspired by such lofty motives. One text makes this abundantly clear:

דְּאָמַר רַב יְהוּדָה אָמַר רַב:
לְעוֹלָם יַעֲסוֹק אָדָם בַּתּוֹרָה וּבַמִּצְוֹת אַף עַל פִּי שֶׁלֹּא לִשְׁמָהּ
שֶׁמִּתּוֹךְ שֶׁלֹּא לִשְׁמָהּ – בָּא לִשְׁמָהּ

Rav Yehuda said in the name of Rav: A person should always engage in Torah and Mitzvahs even if he doesn't do them for their own sake, because — even if the person engages in them not for their own sake — eventually the person will do them for their own sake.

(Talmud Pesachim 50b)

> **What does it mean "even if one doesn't do them for their own sake"? Who do you think will benefit from the mitzvah? What is the hope that will eventually occur?**

Why Give Tzedakah: Do you agree with the texts?

Circle your answer! Be ready to support your decision!

Even a poor person who receives Tzedakah must give from what he receives.

(Talmud Gittin 7b)

AGREE   **DISAGREE**

If a person sees that his resources are limited, let him use them for Tzedakah – and so much the more so if he has extensive resources.

(Talmud Gitten 7a)

AGREE   **DISAGREE**

One who causes others to give Tzedakah is greater than the giver himself.

(Talmud Bava Batra 9a)

AGREE   **DISAGREE**

A story is told of Binyamin HaTzaddik who was the supervisor of the community's Tzedakah funds. Once, when food was scarce, a woman came to him and said, "Rabbi, feed me!" He replied, "I swear there is nothing in the Tzedakah fund." She said, "If you do not feed me, a woman and her seven children will die." So he fed her from his own money.

(Talmud Bava Batra 11a)

AGREE
BINYAMIN'S ACTIONS

DISAGREE WITH
BINYAMIN'S ACTIONS

Would you have done the same thing as Binyamin HaTzaddik?

Motives for Giving Tzedakah

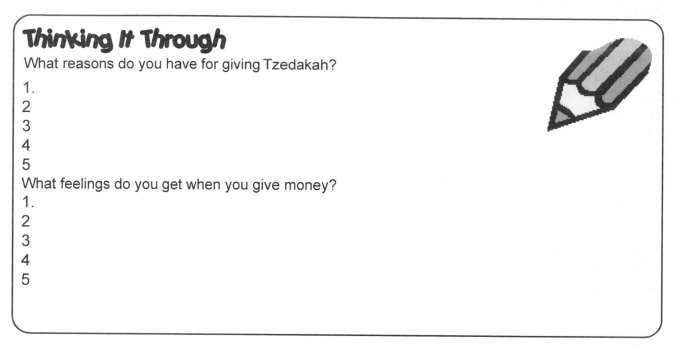

Thinking It Through

What reasons do you have for giving Tzedakah?

1.
2
3
4
5

What feelings do you get when you give money?

1.
2
3
4
5

What follows is a more detailed review of some of the many other possible conscious or unconscious reasons for your generosity:

Accomplishment I: You may like the sense of accomplishment. Giving Tzedakah is, for lack of a better term, very "real". You have not only thought about or theorized about "the significance of action" in a philosophical context, but you have also done something, some Mitzvah, that you can actually feel. That act of Tzedakah touches life, the world outside of yourself, and your internal being. Your sense of accomplishment is rooted in the feeling that you are not helpless in the face of the ostensibly insurmountable troubles, sadness, and human woe in the world. You can change lives for the better.

Accomplishment II: Think of the many times you have said "This made my day." You can pinpoint some moment that stood out as having greater significance than all of the other moments of the day. It may well be that some weird circumstance "makes your day". For example, your distant cousin, two years younger than yourself has been called to Paradise. Totally unexpectedly, a codicil to the will states, "…and I leave my 17-room mansion in Westchester and every nickel in my on-shore and off-shore bank accounts to my dear

cousin Heschie." Total value: $43,000,000 after all taxes are paid. And this is the cousin you used to taunt with nicknames like "fatty" or "doofus". In fact, it was perfect timing, as you were close to actually leaving the job you have hated for 10 years, even though no new employment opportunities were on the horizon. I suppose that kind of thing would "make your day", though the odds of that actually happening are approximately slim-to-zero. On the other hand, giving Tzedakah has the ability to "make your day" every time you do it.

"Connectedness": You feel connected. With an act of Tzedakah you are neither alone nor lonely. You are attached to others — to other human beings who share your common human sense of fear, sadness, pain, and joy. You are linked to others wherever they may be on the face of the earth. You are attached to the past, because for more than three millennia Jewish tradition has taught that this is how you should respond to the needs of others. You are linked to the present, because you are doing something for others that happens now. And you are a part of their future, whether it is the kid who has no family who goes to camp because of your Tzedakah money or the infant car seat you provided to a single mother who has no money to buy one. Whatever the specific situation, your future and theirs are forever bound one to another.

Power: You are aware of how power can be abusive and is abused. Leafing through even a few pages of a newspaper or catching three minutes on the nightly news causes you distress. Simultaneously, you know that the right kind of power can be a great human blessing. You may feel that in your heart, mind, and soul, and in your bones. Any thoughts of being helpless or trapped have been dismissed from your mind. You can change the way things are.

Self-image: The prior descriptions make you feel good about yourself. You know you are somebody because your acts of Tzedakah have done so much for others. Social workers and every kind of therapist are often called upon to work with individuals who have lost their self-image. These specialists have developed many fine methods for dealing with a person's broken, battered, suppressed, or lost self-esteem. Every day, the therapists build and re-build their clients' bruised self image. Time and again, the same holds true for concerned classroom teachers, camp counselors, and sports coaches. Each one, in turn, uses his or her own skills to allow the patients, students, players, wards, and campers to develop fully as human beings with a solid, stable, and resilient feeling of self-worth. Giving Tzedakah can serve as a constant reminder that you are someone of value. I would certainly add Mitzvah heroes to the list of healers. These are individuals who, through their grand Tzedakah work teach, train, and encourage others to become Mitzvah People. As mentioned throughout this book, Mitzvah heroes are distinguished teachers in the field of Tzedakah, Mitzvahs, and Tikun Olam. They know intimately how very great the power of Tzedakah is to remind others that they are somebody. And not only that they are somebody, but somebody of great value both to themselves as well as to others. Tzedakah opportunities are so numerous and varied, Mitzvah heroes know that there is an appropriate match for every individual. And just as a therapist designs a plan of treatment according to the needs of each individual patient, so, too, Mitzvah heroes use their skills to make the best possible match. Whatever scale is used to measure improvement in self-image, empirical studies demonstrate that Tzedakah is extremely effective.

Stability: It is true that some people thrive on chaos. Biographies and autobiographies of many artists, musicians, authors, and poets give eloquent testimony to that fact-of-life. You may simply need stability in your life. You are not extreme about this and don't display any characteristics of being a control freak. However, some degree of order and orderliness allows you to function well. Giving Tzedakah, as well as doing Deeds of Goodness and Kindness with your time can bring order out of chaos. This is particularly true if you have established a regular habit of giving.

Meaning in Life: Giving Tzedakah might possibly give meaning to your life.

Feeling Good: Earlier in this chapter I mentioned "feeling good about yourself" and how giving Tzedakah may lead you to that frame of mind. I think that there is an even more basic feeling which Tzedakah touches very deeply: just plain feeling good. Your ability to feel good about yourself depends on genetics, accident, upbringing, environment, happenstance, possible psychosomatic elements, and a mile-long list of other factors. The same is true for your "unhappiness threshold". What is clear, however, is that you would prefer to feel good rather than bad. Giving Tzedakah most definitely can be a contributing factor to good feelings. The Talmud records an interesting statement by Rabbi Yehoshua ben Levi:

אמר רבי יהושע בן לוי...
חש בגרונו...חש במעיו...חש בעצמותיו...
חש בכל גופו...חש בראשו —
יעסוק בתורה

If you have a headache..., a sore throat..., a stomach ache..., a pain in your bones..., pain in your entire body — study Torah.

(Talmud Eruvin 54a)

Many interpretations have been given, some medically and psychologically valid, others rather farfetched. Two excellent comments I have heard are that (1) studying Torah takes your mind off your pain, and (2) because Torah study is of such great importance to you, it can elevate you above your pain. I would think that what is true for Torah study would certainly be true for giving Tzedakah. As you do your Tzedakah giving, many "Woe is me!" thoughts can fade into the back of your consciousness. Though you do not feel well because of some physical pain, you can still feel good.

To summarize: On the one hand, Mitzvahs are Mitzvahs, and doing them for sublime reasons is a most worthy approach. In the final analysis, however, any and all of the other motivations produce great benefits for both the recipient and the giver, and that really is what is most important. The world is a better place; people in need feel better; they have food, warmth, a roof over their heads, and they live with greater dignity — all because of the power of the Mitzvah of Tzedakah. And you, by using your Tzedakah money wisely, most definitely also feel very good. It is a true win-win life situation.

Challenges of Tzedakah

Thinking It Through

1) When I have a lot of money in my pocket, I _____

_____ .

2) When my friends are talking and someone brings up money, I feel _____

_____ .

3) Why do you think some people may find it difficult to talk about money?

Did the Rabbis from Ancient and Medieval times really understand "real life" when they established the rules for giving tzedakah?

כל האיברים תלוין בלב והלב תלוי בכיס

Every part of the human body depends on the heart,
But the heart depends on the pocket.

(Jerusalem Talmud, Terumot 8:10)

א"ר יוחנן כיפה של חשבונות היתה חוץ לירושלים
וכל מי שמבקש לחשב הולך לשם
למה שלא יחשב בירושלים ויצר
לפי שנקרא משוש כל הארץ

Rabbi Yochanan said:
The arcade of [Jerusalem's] accountants' offices was outside the city limits of Jerusalem. Whoever wanted to review his or her accounts would go there.
Why [were the accountants' offices outside of the city]?
In case a person would become depressed while reviewing the accounts — [and being depressed would contradict the very nature of Jerusalem] which is called "The Joy of the Entire Earth."

(Exodus Rabba, end of Pekudai, based upon Psalm 48:3)

Two Jewish texts written on the previous page should give us some insight:

It is easy to be lyrical about the amazing power of Tzedakah. Tzedakah done in the correct way elicits words and half-words that are heavily charged with emotion. "Awesome", "Incredible!", "Ah!", and "Wow!" are only three of the reactions you may have when you watch Tzedakah work its wonders. That is how it should be. The poetic level of Tzedakah allows you to not only know but also to feel that life can be very rich and beautiful. Yet, you live your life day-to-day, hour-by-hour, and minute-by-minute, and most of your time is extremely prosaic. The first text in this chapter is a very realistic reminder that, without money, you cannot even have the most basic essentials you need to live. The heart — seat of emotions, personality, aspirations, and dreams — simply won't function unless there is money in the pocket to feed, provide warmth for, and shelter your human body.

Similarly, it is easy to be lyrical about ירושלים—Jerusalem. It is the City of Holiness, capital of our Jewish homeland, a geographical point that is more than just another place on the map. Jerusalem is also known in our tradition as משוש כל הארץ—The Joy of the Entire World. (Psalm 48:3) As strange as it sounds, the implication is that you are required to be joyous when you are in Jerusalem. I know that there are people who say you can't force people to feel a certain way, but the fact is that Rabbi Yochanan thought that you could.

Let's analyze the text on the previous page:

1) On the one hand, Rabbi Yochanan was fully aware of Jerusalem's awe inspiring character.

2) He also knew the great impact paying bills and the rising cost of a liter of milk has on your emotions and consciousness. Holiness is one thing; putting food on the table and keeping your family warm in the chilly, rainy winter in The Holy City is another.

3) Rabbi Yochanan wanted to make certain that living the high spiritual life was a good thing…as long as it was understood that sooner or later you would have to make your way to the accountant's office to keep yourself realistically rooted in "real" life.

4) Even then, Rabbi Yochanan teaches us — do your accounts, worry about numbers and financial stability, but remember that you are going home. When you are back within the city limits, keep some perspective. Live the moment-to-moment with all its mundane concerns; just know that beyond, above, and all around you is a city of holiness and joy.

For Further Thought

1) Did the Rabbis "get" how life is really lived, or were they so caught up in their Torah studies that they had lost touch with the "ordinariness" of daily living?

2) People often think that the early rabbis were not in touch with the reality of life. Does this selection show a connection to the reality of life?

Flex Your Tzedakah Muscles

Use this chart to show what percentage of your personal money you feel you can allocate to Tzedakah.

After you have read through the rest of this book, return to this page to see if you feel you can change your percentages at all.

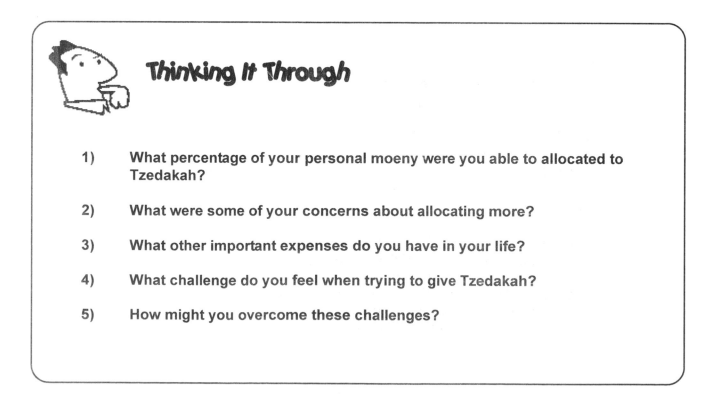

Thinking It Through

1)   What percentage of your personal moeny were you able to allocated to Tzedakah?

2)   What were some of your concerns about allocating more?

3)   What other important expenses do you have in your life?

4)   What challenge do you feel when trying to give Tzedakah?

5)   How might you overcome these challenges?

Collecting & Distributing Tzedakah

Kevod HeAni, which means diginty of a poor person, is such a multi-faceted mitzvah. There are so many components of the mitzvah, that sometimes it is overwhelming to be able to make sense of them. Judaism speaks individually about collecting and distributing Tzedakah , the obligation to give Tzedakah , who should receive Tzedakah, how to give Tzedakah , giving Tzedakah as a community, and even how much to give.

Our Rabbis taught: The Tzedakah fund is collected by two persons (jointly) and distributed by three....

Why do you think this is the case?

... It is collected by two, because any office conferring authority over the community must be filled by at least two persons. It must be distributed by three, on the analogy of money cases [which are handled by a court of three]

Food for the soup kitchen is collected by three and distributed by three...

Why do you think this is the case?

...since it is distributed as soon as it is collected. Food is distributed every day, the monetary (Tzedakah) fund every Friday.

Our Rabbis taught: The collectors of Tzedakah (when collecting) are not permitted to separate from one another, though one may collect at the gate while the other collects at a shop in the same courtyard. If one of them finds money in the street, he should not put it in his pocket but into the Tzedakah box, and take it out again when he comes home.

Our Rabbis taught: If the collectors (still have money but) no poor people to whom to distribute it, they should change the small coins into larger ones with other persons, but not from their own money. If the supervisors of the soup kitchen (have food left over and) no poor people to whom to distribute it, they may sell it to others but not to themselves. In counting out the money collected for Tzedakah, they should not count the coins two at a time, but only one at a time.

(Talmud Bava Batra 8b)
(Laws of Gifts to Poor People, Mishneh Torah 9:5)

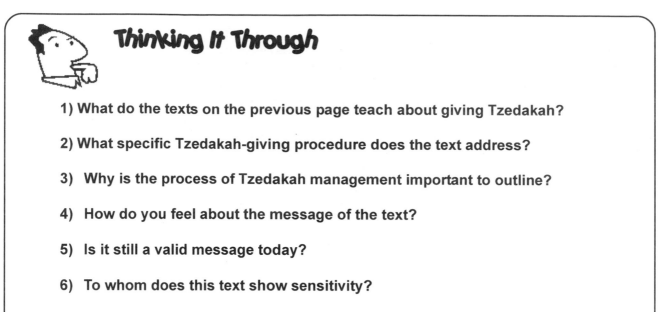

Thinking It Through

1) What do the texts on the previous page teach about giving Tzedakah?

2) What specific Tzedakah-giving procedure does the text address?

3) Why is the process of Tzedakah management important to outline?

4) How do you feel about the message of the text?

5) Is it still a valid message today?

6) To whom does this text show sensitivity?

7) To whom does it show insensitivity?

God Helps Those Who Help Themsleves

Is "God Helps Those Who Help Themselves" a Jewish Principle?
You often hear the phrase "God helps those who help themselves" during a discussion of Tzedakah. Frequently, the implication is that, if people would only work hard, they wouldn't need Tzedakah. Almost as frequently, some will even add "They should pull themselves up by their bootstraps".

What do you think of this concept?

How would you respond?

I would like to examine this aspect of self-help not only from a factual point of view but also from a Jewish perspective — primarily because I have heard the idea expressed with subtle and not-too-subtle negative feelings. The tone of voice will give it away — a slightly patronizing resonance that implies, "I have helped myself fairly well through difficult times — everyone else should be able to do the same." And, unfortunately, sometimes these words are uttered by non-givers or minimal-givers.

Let us take a closer look at this approach to Tikun Olam: In reality, while there are people who can help themselves, there are many "classes" of people who cannot help themselves — people with Alzheimer's, people in periods of history like the Great Depression who searched for jobs when there were none to be had, individuals with such severe disabilities they cannot function on their own, children and adults lying in hospitals intubated and monitored and unable to pay their medical bills. That is barely the beginning of even "the short list".

The appropriate Jewish response would be: We must use our resources to assure their physical, emotional, and spiritual well-being. And as much as we would like it to be done exclusively by human acts of Gemillut Chassadim — acts of caring, lovingkindness — it frequently takes money, Tzedakah money, to make it happen.

There are others, of course, who might be able to "help themselves", but setbacks of every kind and every degree may have stalled them: Natural disaster has demolished all their worldly possessions, corrupt corporate officials have wiped out their retirement accounts, batterers have forced spouses and children to flee the home with nothing but the clothes on their backs, freak accidents have caused severe injury. Again, this is just the beginning of even "the short list". The appropriate Jewish response would be: We must use our resources to assure their physical, emotional, and spiritual well-being and to work with them to re-establish their stability and their ability to function with some greater degree of independence. Many Tzedakah organizations are devoted to just that aspect of Tikun Olam — job training agencies, "business clothing" groups that provide individuals with proper attire for job interviews, social workers at shelters for victims of domestic violence, youth workers dedicated to getting kids out of gangs. And as much as we would like it to be done by human acts of Gemilut Chassadim, acts of caring or lovingkindness, it often takes money, Tzedakah money, and occasionally large sums of Tzedakah money to make it happen.

Yet another category of people — perhaps the most difficult and troubling for others — needs to be considered. These are individuals-in-need who are unpleasant, "difficult people", sometimes even insufferable and obnoxious in their relationships with others. Feeling helpless when you extend your hand, you might naturally distance yourself from them. Here, too, there is a Jewish response, in two stages:

> First, you should attempt to recall times when you may have been unresponsive or even nasty when others reached out to you. While professional therapists may be able to recognize the reasons for other people's behavior, nonprofessionals are incapable of doing a psychiatric evaluation of why other people act the way they do. We must deal with the immediate situation-at-hand of another human being in need. Reminding ourselves of our own less-than-perfect personality traits lays the groundwork for a practical solution by calling on our sense of רחמנות—Rachmanut, empathy to encourage us to respond in some fashion. It reminds us that there is no "we" and "they", but, rather, that we have something very much in common.

> Secondly, you need to recognize that there are Mitzvah heroes everywhere, "specialists" who are capable of working with these extreme situations. They seem to have the magic human touch (though there is no "magic" to it). Their exceptional sensitivities, tied to tremendous Mitzvah skills, allows the Mitzvah heroes to reach even the most difficult people who would curse or resist in the most distasteful manner any attempts anyone might make to bring them benefit. A practical solution, then, would be to place our Tzedakah money at the disposal of these Mitzvah heroes, allowing them to bring stability, functionality, and well-being to the people they serve.

 Thinking It Through

1) **Have you ever known someon who could not help him/ herself, but who was able to be helped with Tzedakah money?**

2) **Can that experience or story be duplicated with others in your community?**

Systemic Change?

Where Does Change Begin?

1) Shouldn't your primary concern be to make the systematic changes that will eliminate those very conditions that cause people to be in need?

2) Should Tzedakah money only be used for systemic change?

3) What percentage is appropriate for giving for systemic change?

The answer to the first question: Yes. To a certain extent.

For example, The Preamble to the American Constitution expresses the following lofty ideals of American democracy:

"We the People of the United States, in order to form a more perfect Union, establish justice, insure domestic tranquility, provide for the common defense, promote the general welfare, and secure the blessings of lberty to ourselves and our posterity, do ordain and establish this Constitution for the United States of America."

In order to make those ideals a reality in our lives, the system has to be not only constructed properly, but it must also work. When the system is sluggish or dysfunctional, then systemic change is crucial to the entire Tikun Olam context. You only need to consider the far-reaching changes brought about by the Voting Rights Act, the Civil Rights Act, and the Americans with Disabilities Act. All of these required enormous efforts by many people as well as considerable financial resources.

The preceding paragraph describes aspects of the democratic system. Studying socialism, communism, feudalism, fascism and various societal experiments, for example, and comparing and contrasting them, will naturally sharpen your sense of how societies function, and whether or not — even if they function smoothly — they preserve human dignity. As productive, I would think, would be a review of the development and state of the kibbutz in Israel. Why and how kibbutzim were founded, how they developed, and how they dealt with and deal with aging populations, individuals with special needs, and their understanding of Tzedakah and Tikun Olam is very enriching and would possibly contribute greatly to your own personal practice of Tzedakah.

So, yes, working for systemic change, and applying Tzedakah money towards that kind of change is of major importance. But another aspect of Tzedakah remains, the personalized i.e., "in the meantime..." type of Tzedakah. In the meantime, there are people without the most basic human shelter, access to essential health services — even something as simple as aspirin, who go days without food and have no hope for any in the immediate future. Not only does this kind of basic Tzedakah provide immediate relief, it often leads many people to find systemic solutions for those very needs that they have discovered when giving.

There are really two ways to arrive at systemic solutions:

(1) theoretical thinking, whereby experts in societal structure and function study the system and then offer possible solutions for the world's ills, and

(2) front-line Tzedakah work, which leads to creative all-encompassing change. In and of itself, neither approach is sufficient to bring us to a just and fair world. Both approaches complement each other. However, I sense that the better, more long-lasting solutions originate with Tzedakah work that is, as it were, in the trenches of mud, filth, mental confusion on either side of the line of madness, bone-chilling cold, and the rumbling stomachs of schoolchildren whether they are in Afula, Detroit, or Minsk, who want to learn math, literature, and history, but haven't had breakfast.

A regular pattern of personalized Tzedakah that deals constantly with the needs of real people provides an ever-present reminder that you are involved in the lives of human beings with very real needs. Solutions demand a measure of childhood naïveté that sometimes sees the world without the muddling interference of over-intellectualizing. And, as well, solutions demand sophisticated adult reasoning, power, and ability to connect resources to needs. How much of which you, yourself, will use, depends on your own personality. Whatever you choose as best for yourself, once personalized, Tzedakah will saturate every aspect of your Mitzvah work. As a result, you may very well be led to a clearer vision of full, even ultimate, Tikun Olam solutions.

Thinking It Through

1) Do you feel that there is a need to only make changes that are systemic? Why or why not?

2) What would you want to change if you could?

3) How could you use your money to change it?

Whose Money Is It?

Tzedakah Scenarios

Choose one of the following scenarios:

Scenario One:
Your parents have decided to give you a weekly allowance. They have asked for your opinion to determine how much you should receive. Think about how much you would "require" for your needs, and how you would spend the money. What would you ask your parents for? What do you think you would use the money for?

Scenario Two:
You just got a job at the mall at one of the new music stores that just opened. You are excited about the job because not only is it a great way to spend your afternoons, but you'll now bring home a paycheck every week. How much do you think you would need in order to cover your weekly expenses? How would you spend your money?

Does Tzedakah Money Really Belong to You?

How much money do you require for your personal needs?

How much Tzedakah money do they need?

קונם כהנים ולוים נהנים לי יטלו על כרחו

[If a farmer says,] "I vow that the כהנים—Kohanim, Priests and לוים—Levi'im, Levites should have no benefit of anything that is mine, they may still take, even against the farmer's will.

(Mishnah Nedarim 11:3)

In Biblical times, farmers had certain obligations to use a part of their crops for Tzedakah. Among the types of Mitzvah-produce designated for poor people were:

לקט—Leket, gleanings, food which fell during harvest.
פאה—Pe'ah, the corners of the field to be left uncut.
שכחה—Shichecha, areas the farmer forgot to reap.

In addition, there were special portions set aside for the Priests and Levites:

תרומה—Terumah for the Priests
מעשר—Ma'aser for the Levites

If the farmer believes it's his land, why can't he do what he wants with it?

Some of the rules of distribution and their underlying principles includes:

1.   Even if the farmer solemnly vows not to give Terumah and Ma'aser, the Kohanim and Levi'im can *still* take the Terumah and Ma'aser, because they *rightfully* belong to them. This is clearly stated in the Mishnah at the beginning of this chapter.

2.   This means that Terumah and Ma'aser never really belonged to the farmer.

3.   Consequently, the farmer cannot refuse to give them to the Kohanim and Levi'im.

4.   In certain situations, the farmer may designate *which* Kohanim and Levi'im may re ceive the Terumah and Ma'aser.

5.   No matter which specific Kohanim or Levi'im the farmer designates, it still *must* be set aside.

6.   The farmer is not even allowed to use the rest of the crop for personal needs until the Terumah and Ma'aser have been set aside,

Other Jewish texts support this position concerning what you really own and what you do not own. Tzedakah money doesn't belong to you to begin with, and rather than viewing yourself as sharing what you own, you are asked to understand that you are a trustee — God's trustee — over this percentage of your money. As a trustee, agent, and partner-with-God, you therefore have the sacred. On one hand, it is an awesome, perhaps overpowering thought to be God's partner. It is certainly very humbling. But on the other hand, it is very empowering to know that there is a distinctly Divine element in the act of Tzedakah.

Thus, in Jewish life, there really are two kinds of money — money for your own personal use, and Tzedakah money, which is money to be used for the good of other people.

Many questions that apply to your own money also apply to Tzedakah. The two most crucial questions are:

1. "Yours" — How much money do you require for your personal needs?

2. "Theirs" — How much Tzedakah money do they need?

The more you think of "yours" and "theirs", the more you will observe different categories of people and how they relate to money.

1. "Yours" — In the extreme, some people live as if there is never enough money in their account and always crave more. They may consider a 10-room house on five acres of land insufficient for a two-person household. A friend of mine once called this "living large".

2. "Theirs" — At the other end of the people-and-money scale, some people never stop wanting more Tzedakah money to accomplish that much more Tikun Olam. Instead of having X dollars to distribute, they wish that they had 10 times X Tzedakah dollars or X to the 10th power of Tzedakah dollars at their disposal. They "live large" through their giving, insisting on doing the Mitzvah with an extra-generous touch. This is known as "הידור מצוה-Hiddur Mitzvah", Doing a Mitzvah Beautifully.

3. "Yours and theirs" — Another one of my friends said it succinctly and eloquently, "If you live large, give large."

The distance between the two extremes is very great. Most people are somewhere in the middle.

Where do you think you fit in?

You may know a few people who are so successful that they have a winter beachfront mansion on Maui and a ski chalet in Utah who still want more and more and always more. You have certainly observed their lifestyles in the media, but most likely, they are not your "main crowd". There is even a slight chance that you, yourself, are one of the "never enough" people.

You may be one of those who doesn't happen to book the penthouse suite at the Plaza Hotel in New York or doesn't happen to have umpteen thousands of shares of stock in your portfolio. You may be just plain old middle class, living well within your means while worrying about meeting the next college tuition payment. But you consciously and frequently let your mind wander to thoughts like, "If I only had $10,000,000 for Tzedakah." Good. That's a very healthy approach to "yours" and "theirs" money.

You may be fortunate to know several people who have a private jet, $3,000 suits, and a landscape architect on retainer to re-design their grounds at their slightest whim — but who are generous-to-the-extreme (in the most positive sense) with their Tzedakah money. They live large and give large. You may be one yourself. You are living large and giving large.

Exercise:
What makes Tzedakah a "Jewish" activity?

On a scale of 1-10 rate the following, 10 being the most or highest.
Explain your ratings:

1. How important to you is doing Tzedakah Jewishly?
1 _____ 10
Explain:

2. Do you think that Tzedakah is a religious obligation (1) or a human obligation (10)?
1 _____ 10
Explain:

3. Do you give Tzedakah because it makes you feel good (1) or because you think it is right? (10)?
1 _____ 10
Explain:

4. How important to you is being Jewish and living Jewishly?
1 _____ 10
Explain:

5. Do you expect that your Tzedakah work will affect your connection, affiliation, and/or commitment to Judaism?
1 _____ 10
Explain:

6. Does doing Tzedakah feel "Jewish" in the same way as keeping Shabbat, keeping Kosher, or praying?
1 _____ 10
Explain:

7. Do you believe that doing Tzedakah is sufficient to keep you connected, affiliated, and/or committed to your Judaism?
1 _____ 10
If your rating is between 6-10, explain below, but if your answer is between 1-5, please move to the next question.
Explain:

(More on Next Page)

8. If your rating for Question #7 was between 1-5, what else do you believe you would have to do to keep your connection, affiliation, and/or commitment to Judaism strong?
Explain:

9. How important is it to you that your descendants *remain* Jewish?
1 _____ 10
Explain:

10. Do you expect that your doing Tzedakah Jewishly will contribute to your descendants' remaining Jewishly connected, affiliated, and/or committed to their Judaism?
1 _____ 10
Explain:

11. If someone asked you why you give Tzedakah, how likely would you be to answer "because it is a religious obligation?"
1 _____ 10
Explain:

12. Do you believe that your doing Tzedakah *is sufficient* to keep your descendants committed to their degree of "Jewishness"?
1 _____ 10
If your rating is between 6-10, explain below, but if your answer is between 1-5, please move to the next question.
Explain:

12. If your rating for Question #12 is between 1-5, what else do you believe you would have to do to influence their Jewish connection, affiliation, and/or commitment to their Judaism?
Explain:

1. Find some useful short quote that you can memorize that will allow you to be constantly aware of the "yours" and "theirs" of money. I personally think that Winston Churchill's quote is one of the best: "We make a living by what we get, but we make a life by what we give."

2. Calculate where you are at present on this "yours" and "theirs" scale, and every so often review the results. Make a note of all the changes that have occurred over time.

YOURS _____ THEIRS

Most of all, whatever you do — do as much of "theirs" as you can.

Doing Tzedakah Jewishly

Judaism offers many ways to do Tzedakah. Several of the principles, values, techniques, and strategies are unique to Jewish tradition. In addition, while it is true that some of the fundamental concepts may have elements common to other systems of giving, Judaism places a different emphasis on those concepts. Furthermore, the organic and dynamic interplay of the Jewish concepts with acts of Tikun Olam provides a distinct approach to discovering the real needs of others. The Jewish way of giving becomes most evident when you examine exactly how these needs are to be met.

"Doing Tzedakah Jewishly" involves two essential elements:

(1) Giving your money away according to distinctly Jewish values and guidelines, and

(2) Your actual Tzedakah decisions, i.e., how much you give to Jewish programs and how much to general programs.

1. Unique Jewish values and practices relating to Tzedakah are discussed throughout this guide. Jewish guidelines for proper Tzedakah giving are as necessary to a civilized, ordered society as traffic laws, fire codes, and fair rental contracts. Tzedakah directives are established to allow you, the giver, to be more efficient in your desire to benefit others. You should be able to easily integrate Jewish practices into contemporary life, American laws, and the latest electronic tools such as e-mail and the internet. Most important, once you are familiar with Judaism's procedures and rules, you will find that there is vast room for individuality and creativity in your own giving. You can work behind the scenes, "on the front lines", or do some combination of both. Whichever way you do it, you should never have reason to doubt that you are making a difference.

2. Thousands of years of Jewish experience should offer guidance as you consider how much to give to Jewish needs and how much to needs beyond the Jewish community. Among several factors to consider are:

Local vs. Global

A. Jewish tradition does not provide an absolute, easy-to-follow "chart" which outlines, "12% to this category of needs, 9% to that type of program, etc." For example, some texts teach that Tzedakah's first priority is saving lives. Other passages in traditional Jewish literature give precedence to local needs in contrast to those far away. Still others stress the priority of Israel's needs, redeeming captives, supporting Torah study, as well as giving to Jewish and/or non-Jewish needs. All of these texts indicate that their recipients should be the most important beneficiaries of Tzedakah. I have found no clear text that ties all of these positions together and gives an authoritative list of "first priorities".

National Disasters?

B. Jewish tradition certainly allows and, indeed, encourages contributing to causes and needs beyond the Jewish community, as exemplified by the outpouring of funds for victims of the September 11, 2001 attacks, the devastating hurricanes of 2005, and for the survivors of the 2004 Asian tsunami.

C. It would be important to learn:

(1) How much money non-Jewish organizations and individuals give to support Jewish needs.

(2) It would also be helpful to review recent studies about the children and grand-children of wealthy Jews who have inherited enormous sums of money. These studies reveal a disturbing trend: While the descendants may continue to con-tribute the same absolute amount of Tzedakah dollars as their parents or grand-parents, they are giving significantly smaller percentages to Jewish needs. These factors should also help you determine how much Tzedakah from Jewish people is needed to provide for the needs of the Jewish community.

(3) You will want to review the overall and the specific needs of the various organi-zations benefiting the Jewish community. As described elsewhere in this guide, for Jewish Tikun Olam programs that particularly appeal to you, you will want to research how efficiently they accomplish their goals.

Jewish vs. Non-Jewish

Do I first give to Israel?

D. The uniquely crucial needs of Israel and its people. In your own giving, you will want to consider how much your own support will make a difference.

Later in this book, we will look closer at the allocations process.

Exercise

If you had $100 to give out to the following different types of organizations*, how do you think you should divide it up?

Organization One: Martha's Food Pantry: An organization in your community which feeds people who are hungry.

Organization Two: Katrina's Heroes: An orga-nization in Louisiana which collects canned foods for distribution to Katrina's victims who are still unable to buy food on their own.

Organization Three: Halav U'D'vash: A local organization which collects Tzedakah funds to provide lunches for Jewish school children who can not otherwise afford to bring food.

Organization Four: Yad L'Yisrael: An organiza-tion in Israel which feeds people who are hun-gry.

(*All organizations listed above are created for the purpose of this exercise.)

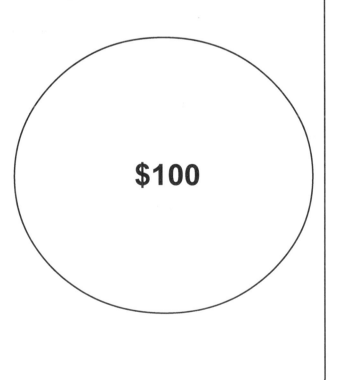

---

34   צדקה–Tzedakah: A Time For Change

Your Jewish Identity

Most likely, your own sense of Jewish identity will largely determine both to what degree you give Jewishly and how much you give to Jewish Tzedakah programs. Regardless of how you identify with your Jewishness, it is important to remember that there is no need to feel defensive about giving to Jewish needs. Being Jewish, it is natural for you to care about your own, and to act to assure the well-being of your own. Native Americans are not defensive about supporting the needs of Native Americans. The same is true for African Americans and other ethnic, racial, or religious groups. While there are advocates of strictly universalistic giving, every group still donates to programs with which they have common ties. "Particularistic" Tzedakah is perfectly acceptable. The following three quotes may help you articulate the suitability of your "particularistic" choices:

1. Solomon Schechter, one of the great Jewish scholars and leaders of the Conservative Movement in the early 20th century, wrote, "We can no more have Jews without Judaism, than Judaism without Jews. We Jews have proven that we can survive difference, but not indifference."

2. In one of his sermons, my teacher, Rabbi Saul Teplitz, wrote, "Often, one finds a phrase on theater tickets that reads: 'Void if detached.' So, too, Jewish life becomes void when it is detached from the practices and principles of Judaism, from synagogue and prayer, from Torah and study." Rabbi Teplitz and I have discussed this, and he most certainly agreed that his list should include "and doing Tzedakah as Jews and for Jews."

3. Finally, returning to our early classic Jewish sources, Hillel's famous words certainly come to mind:

   הוא היה אומר אם אין אני לי מי לי וכשאני לעצמי מה אני

   Reversing the order of Hillel's phrases, I translate:
   "If I am only for myself, what am I?
   But if I am not for myself as well, who will be for me?"
   (Mishnah Pirkei Avot, Chapter 1:14)

To summarize: "Doing Tzedakah Jewishly" encompasses two important features:

(1)   You will want to absorb the unique Jewish material on Tzedakah by whatever method of study you do best.

(2)   How you understand your own Jewish identity will display itself in the practices and emphases of your own Tzedakah giving.

Is There Enough Money?

Is there enough money to do it all?

וְאָמַר רַבִּי יִצְחָק....
כָּל הָרוֹדֵף אַחַר צְדָקָה
הַקָּדוֹשׁ בָּרוּךְ הוּא מַמְצִיא לוֹ מָעוֹת וְעוֹשֶׂה בָהֶן צְדָקָה
רַב נַחְמָן בַּר יִצְחָק אָמַר
הַקָּדוֹשׁ בָּרוּךְ הוּא מַמְצִיא לוֹ בְּנֵי אָדָם הַמְהוּגָנִים
לַעֲשׂוֹת לָהֶן צְדָקָה

Rabbi Yitzchak said...:
The Holy One will provide sufficient money
for any who runs to do Tzedakah.
Rabbi Nachman bar Yitzchak said:
The Holy One will provide appropriate recipients
through whom to perform the Mitzvah of Tzedakah.

(Talmud Bava Batra 9b)

Rabbi Yitzchak's words reveal Judaism's optimistic approach to Tzedakah. If you are willing to take the first step with your money, you can be certain that you will find more money to do Tzedakah. Either others will be moved by your act of Tzedakah and will contribute, or you will find that you, yourselves, actually can manage to give away more than you had originally thought possible. Or both will happen.

Rabbi Nachman bar Yitzchak adds another encouraging element, namely, that your Tzedakah money will not go to waste. There are several techniques that you can learn in order to help you find the appropriate recipients. Most of them are no more difficult than how to turn on a TV or to make a bowl of instant oatmeal. These techniques constitute a significant portion of this guide.

Thinking It Through

בָּרוּךְ אַתָּה יְיָ, אֱלֹהֵינוּ מֶלֶךְ הָעוֹלָם, הַזָּן אֶת הָעוֹלָם כֻּלּוֹ בְּטוּבוֹ בְּחֵן בְּחֶסֶד וּבְרַחֲמִים, הוּא נוֹתֵן לֶחֶם לְכָל בָּשָׂר כִּי לְעוֹלָם חַסְדּוֹ. וּבְטוּבוֹ הַגָּדוֹל תָּמִיד לֹא חָסַר לָנוּ, וְאַל יֶחְסַר לָנוּ מָזוֹן לְעוֹלָם וָעֶד. בַּעֲבוּר שְׁמוֹ הַגָּדוֹל, כִּי הוּא אֵל זָן וּמְפַרְנֵס לַכֹּל וּמֵטִיב לַכֹּל, וּמֵכִין מָזוֹן לְכָל בְּרִיּוֹתָיו אֲשֶׁר בָּרָא. בָּרוּךְ אַתָּה יְיָ, הַזָּן אֶת הַכֹּל.

In Birkat Hamazon (the blessing after meals), we say:

"We praise You, Lord our God, King of the universe who graciously sustains the whole world with kindness and compassion. You provide food for every creature, as Your love endures forever. Your great goodness has never failed us; May Your great glory always assure us nourishment. You sustain all life and You are good to all, providing all of Your creatures with food and sustenance. We praise You, Lord who sustains all life.

How can we recite this bracha, if there are people in the world who are starving?

Is it simply a matter of allocating resources? (Food, money, etc?)

What do you think can or should be done?

If I had a Million Dollars...

You have no rich relatives who love you dearly enough to want to surprise you one day with a check for $1,000,000. You have no relatives left from whom there is the most remote chance you might inherit $1,000,000. There was a TV show years ago called "The Millionaire" where a certain very rich man, John Bearsford Tipton, would anonymously send off a $1,000,000 check to someone he had selected — just to see what the person would do with so much money...but that was only television, and it hasn't been on for years.

This leaves you only one other possibility — winning the lottery. You have dreamed and day-dreamed about it for years. If you won the lottery, say anywhere from $1,000,000 to $45,000,000 —

1. Humorous answers for those people who say, "Jonathan, I know you well enough. If you won the lottery, your lifestyle wouldn't change at all, right?"

2. In what ways would having all this money give you more free time to do more Tikun Olam (in addition to having tons of Tzedakah money to give away)?

3. What percentage of the winnings would you use for yourself?

4. What percentage of the take would you use for Tikun Olam?

5. Of this percentage, how much would you give away (secretly) in hard cash to people in need, since that is exactly what they might need at that point in life to regain their financial stability—even small amounts of Tzedakah? Why do you think "hard cash" might be important?

6. Would you give it all to one "cause", i.e. one portion of Tikun Olam, or would you use it for many areas of Mitzvah work, as long as each Tzedakah dollar made a difference?

7. Explain your answer for question #6.

8. What percentage would you donate to an interest-free loan society that would lend out the money, receive it back in re-payments, then lend it out again, achieving thereby more "bang for the Tzedakah-dollar"?

9. Would you give it all to one Mitzvah hero to end, once and for all, any financial worries she or he might have, so that she or he can be free to do just do what has to be done for Tikun Olam?

(Exercise continues on next page)

10. If so, why, and if not, why not?

11. Would you start your own organization or foundation?
    Circle your answer:
    YES   NO

12. If so, why? To do what?

13. If not, why not?

14. Now assume that you didn't win the lottery. How would you respond to questions all of the questions you just answered?

לעולם אין אדם מעני מן הצדקה
ואין דבר רע ולא היזק נגלל בשביל הצדקה
שנאמר והיה מעשה הצדקה שלום

No one ever becomes poor from doing Tzedakah.
Nothing bad or harmful comes from doing Tzedakah,
as the verse states,
"The end result of Tzedakah will be peace,
and Tzedakah work will yield
eternal peace-of-mind and security."
(Maimonides, Hilchot Matnot Ani'im [The Laws of Gifts to Poor People] 10:2, Isaiah 32:17)

---

2 Part Two: Practical Guide to Giving Tzedakah

Tzedakah On Your Brain

Make a list of 10 things that you can do to make Tzedakah giving a priority in your life.

1. *Put a Tzedakah Box (Pushka) by your front door*
2
3
4
5
6
7
8
9
10

Techniques for Raising your Tzedakah Awareness

The end of the secular calendar year is "high time" for Tzedakah donations. It is the last chance for donors to review their Tzedakah contributions for tax purposes. Some people do all of their Tzedakah at that time, but many are uncomfortable with this once-a-year method. They understand that because of a sudden cold wave in October, some immediate need has to be addressed, or they are aware that giving frequently during the course of the year gives them a sense of Tzedakah as a regular practice, part of their "normal" life. In no particular order, the following are a few suggestions for keeping Tzedakah in the forefront of both your Tzedakah thinking and your Tzedakah doing.

1. Tzedakah boxes (pushkas)
   a. Keep several Tzedakah boxes (pushkas) around your house. This will provide you with many more opportunities to visually remember to do Tzedakah.

   b. Keep a Tzedakah box near the washing machine for all the loose coins and the occasional bills that you might find in pockets.

   c. Periodically check under the cushions of couches and easy chairs. They are likely treasure troves of Tzedakah money.

d. Empty your loose change at the end of the day into the pushka. One friend was delighted when his apartment building changed the washers and driers from quarters to a magnetic card. That "liberated" considerably more money — quarters galore — for his pushka.

e. Periodically estimate by weight how much has accumulated. This stimulates yet another of the five senses to the importance of Tzedakah.

f. At regular intervals, count the accumulated coins and bills. For the coins — resist the temptation to use a bank's automatic counting machine. Pouring all the coins into a machine in a huge rush and immediately reading the total on a screen tends to dull the sense of how coins add up to significant amounts of money for Tikun Olam. Do it the old-fashioned way: Count everything slowly and carefully and roll them into packages to take to the bank.

g. Every so often, create your own pushka. Some people prefer to make see-through Tzedakah boxes so that they can watch the Tzedakah money grow. Others prefer any material that prevents seeing how much has accumulated. They prefer the surprise and delight of the slowly-growing total as they sort and count the coins and bills.

h. Put other "found money", such as coins you might find on the sidewalk — in the pushka. The late Rabbi Richard Israel, ז״ל, was a long-distance runner. Every year, Ziv Tzedakah Fund would receive a check representing a sizable amount of money he had found during his hundreds of miles of jogging.

2. Put a reminder in your phone or PDA to give Tzedakah some time every day. Choose your own best option: to flash on the screen periodically during the day, to have a sound alarm go off first thing in the morning, to design a graphic that will bring the message home to yourself. *Whatever works best for you.*

3. Holidays and Shabbat: Before lighting candles on Friday and before holidays, put some money in a Tzedakah box. Tying Tzedakah to this beautiful ritual of light can be very powerful; juxtaposing the two gives greater significance to both the sacred time of Shabbat and holidays and to Tzedakah.

   a. Purim has a special name for its specific Mitzvah of Tzedakah — Matanot LaEvyonim-מתנות לאביונים (Gifts to Poor People). On this particularly joyous and fun day, you would want to make sure that everyone can join in the fun, including having a fine holiday meal.

   b. Passover has two terms for its own Tzedakah, one in Hebrew and one in Aramaic: Ma'ot Chittin-מעות חטין, Money for Wheat and Kimcha DePischa-קימחא דפיסחא, [Money for] Passover Flour. Both of them mean "to donate money so that people who cannot afford Matzah will be able to have it".

   d. On Yom Kippur and other fast days, the money you would have spent on your own meals were you not fasting is to go to Tzedakah. As the Talmudic Rabbi Mar Zutra taught hundreds of years ago: אגרא דתעניתא צדקתא— the reward for fasting is Tzedakah. (Brachot 6b) I find the term "אגרא-agra", reward, a very interesting choice of words on Mar Zutra's part. Why a reward? I have heard several interpretations, one of which makes the most sense to me in the framework of Talmudic thinking: If fasting is meant as a vehicle to help you re-orient your sense of values, then Mar Zutra is saying, "Prove your new priorities by doing something for others." The "reward", then, would be that you have had the opportunity to do a Mitzvah.

    e.   Remembering to provide for others before any holiday is another way of making certain that Tzedakah is a frequent part of your cycle of living and giving.

4. Every time you go grocery shopping, buy one extra item for Tzedakah, and deliver the items regularly to the synagogue food box or other agencies' collection points.

5. Open two separate checking accounts, one for Tzedakah and one for personal expenses. Use different-colored checks, and sign both differently (possibly using a middle initial or some other device to remind yourself which is which).

6. As soon as you receive any income–from allowances, part-time jobs, etc., separate the appropriate percentage for Tzedakah and deposit it in the Tzedakah bank account. From your earliest age, you should also get into the habit of separating your money, whether from allowance, money received as presents, or jobs of any kind, no matter how little the amount you receive.

7. Hold regular family meetings to discuss various opportunities for giving. Make sure to listen to your parents. They frequently have ideas and insights that you might miss completely. (And make sure they listen to your ideas too!)

8. Have get-togethers with friends to discuss the needs of others and where your individual or combined Tzedakah may best be used. Form a Tzedakah collective.

9. Create a physical file of newspaper and magazine articles about The Good People who are doing great Tikun Olam work. Similarly, bookmark important Tikun Olam websites for easy reference. Share the stories, lessons, and ideas with your family and circle of friends.

10. Daydream often.
    a.   If it is a cloudy day, imagine seeing a humongous pushka in the sky.

    b.   Imagine winning the lottery. Calculate what you would do for Tikun Olam with a percentage of those millions of dollars.

Of course, if you are always on the look-out for Tzedakah opportunities, all of the above will come naturally to you. In retrospect, most likely #1-10 will seem like a very short list, and you will discover that you may not even need reminders at all.

Tzedakah Smarts:
Making Wise Decisions About Tzedakah

The Tzedakah Disconnect: Analogies

Consider some of the recommendations in this guide about doing research about a particular Tzedakah program. Most of them are simple and logical.

What questions do you ask when...

1) You want to purchase an expensive item like a new IPOD or video game unit?

2) You are shopping at the mall for new clothing?

3) You are trying to decide which college to attend?

4) You are considering accepting a part-time job offer?

You know what you need; you use various methods to get the proper information; you ask for advice from people who have done it before or otherwise are experts in the field, and, before you make your final decision, you weigh the various options in your mind.

Once all of the above is taken into account — then, and only then, do you commit.

The disconnect is that, when it comes to giving Tzedakah, sometimes some or all of these most elementary steps fall by the wayside. One example — buying a computer — should make this clear. First, is the person selling you the Mac or PC primarily concerned with what your personal needs are? Second, has the salesperson covered everything? Do you do graphics? Compose music? Do slide shows or videos work for business presentations? ...And if not, is he or she trying to sweet-talk you and sell you a bill of goods loaded with things you don't need? Third, is the price — the cost to the dealer and the profit margin — reasonable? And, finally, will this G4 Powerbook laptop really do everything it is supposed to do, and will it do it with no unreasonable need for constant monitoring and repair? All of these questions help you to consider where you are giving your Tzedakah money.

Furthermore, it may even be that sometime in the past you were "burned", as in:

1) The CD you recently bought didn't have complete versions of the songs on it. You were told by the salesman that you could bring it back, but now the store won't let you exchange it.
2) The money-back guarantee didn't apply to your purchase because of a technicality, or
3) You may have fallen for something "too good to be true" which, in fact, turned out to be too good to be true, or
4) When you were interviewing for a new job, the human resources person promised that your supervisor would work closely with you to teach you everything you needed to

know, only to have him or her slough off the responsibility and leave you to muddle your way through the intricate tasks. You learned very quickly, not only in your mind, but also in your gut, that the next time you will need to proceed more carefully, sometimes much more carefully.

Unfortunately, when it comes to Tzedakah, one additional element enters the picture. Again, for three decades I have had conversations on this topic with people of all ages and economic status. All too frequently, I have found that many people more readily abandon Tzedakah altogether after being burned only once or twice. This is a serious problem and one that needs to be addressed by everyone concerned about Tikun Olam.

Tzedakah Thinking

Speech, logic, and physical dexterity originate in distinct locations of the brain. The right half and left half of your brain produce different manifestations of your behavior. Research on both healthy and damaged or diseased brains reveal more answers to age-old mysteries than you could have imagined even 10 years ago. To a certain extent, genes, chemicals, electrical charges, and brain geography in isolation or in interconnection help explain who you are and how you function.

It may be that Tzedakah thinking involves a different part of the brain. It is possible that endorphins and other complex molecular structures are activated when you respond to the cry of a weeping child who has been abused. These same chemicals may be "taking a Shabbat nap" because they are not needed when you tell the mechanic that your car shakes uncontrollably.

With all this talk about Tzedakah thinking, you are probably wondering, "Maybe there are people who are 'Tzedakah-challenged'?" Maybe there is some genetic deficiency or chemical imbalance in the "Tzedakah" area of the brain that would prevent them from doing this vital Mitzvah beautifully, or at all? You may justifiably wonder about that as you consider people who are doing very well and should know better than to keep it all to themselves. Even in those extreme cases, though, and you consider physiologically "Tzedakah-challenged" people, there are teachers who can work with them, just as special needs teachers can help students with dyslexia or dyscalculia.

I would suspect, though, that the issue is not essentially neurological in origin. If there are some people who have TzDS (Tzedakah Deficiency Syndrome), they are rare. There is no reason to assume that you, yourself, and most other people are anything other than medically well within the norm. I think the crux of the matter is this: You may have thought that Tzedakah comes naturally, and that it is something you just automatically know how to do. In my opinion, this is true only to a certain extent. Consider the following two points:

1. Becoming "good at Tzedakah" requires knowledge, training, and practice. Just as there are writing instructors who work with their students to help them write their best prose or poetry, so, too, you can find teachers and advisors who can work with your own talents and sensitivities and allow you to reach your maximum Tzedakah potential.

2. There are some people who seem to have "the natural touch" with Tzedakah and whose very essence is Tzedakah at its best. But even those people who do have the natural touch need to refine their skills. It is no different than a great opera singer who still needs a voice teacher or a home run slugger who works regularly with a batting coach.

Again, in my opinion, skill is skill and the analogies hold. But even if Mitzvah thinking is an altogether different skill, the significant odds are that you can master most, if not all, of it. With elementary or moderate guidance from the right teacher, you will become more proficient at Fixing the World with your Tzedakah money. The right teachers do exist, ones who understand not only the non-profit world and fundraising, but who also understand Tzedakah. They are not difficult to find, and once you begin to search for them, you may be surprised that so many of them exist or even that they exist at all. Remember, too, that they, themselves, have teachers and advisors (Tzedakah Rebbis) when they are confronted with difficult situations that are beyond their own expertise. *Everyone* needs to continue learning about Tzedakah.

Why Some People Give

You most likely want to give Tzedakah because you are concerned for the well-being of others. You sincerely want to do Tikun Olam, to repair some aspect of what is bad, wrong, unjust, broken, or terribly messy in the vast array of things already in isarray or due to fall apart in the future — unless something serious and concrete is ne now. The question then arises, "Why do some people who ostensibly share your it of view still manage to make less-than-wise decisions?" I would begin to answer uggesting that there are several other factors that affect some individuals' (and foundations') decisions, sometimes in a detrimental way. Among them are:

1. Sentimental feelings,
2. A sudden influx of enormous income,
3. The occasion of honoring or memorializing a deceased parent or friend,
4. The need for attention because Mommy and Daddy never thought their child would amount to much in life,
5. A craving for flattery (whatever the psychological roots),
6. The need to repair a damaged reputation,
7. A desire for Kavod (being publicly honored),
8. The desire to keep up with the Cohens, Cohns, Kahns, Kahans, Cahans, or Kagans who are substantial givers,
9. The need to gain entre into an exclusive circle within the community or to meet glitterati,
10. The need to build business connections,
11. The Tzedakah advisor had his or her own interests in mind rather than those of the donor and the recipients,
12. Even an enthusiasm to do something good. This may turn into a hyper or manic enthu siasm, which can cloud the donor's ability to "think" Tzedakah clearly.

All of these factors, alone or in various combinations, may possibly interfere with making sound Tzedakah decisions.

To illustrate — #2, "a sudden influx of enormous income":
My long-time friend, Marc Pollick, established The Giving Back Fund because he saw a very real donor's need. He noticed that there were many stars, celebrities, and other high-profile people who needed to sharpen their Tzedakah skills and leverage their fame to bring about greater Tikun Olam. The fund (www.givingback.org) has many programs, but I remember one particularly sensible example that Marc mentioned in one of our conversations.

He explained:

Take a young basketball star, maybe 21 years old and fresh out of college.  He is getting a $7,000,000-a-year salary for five years, plus a $2,500,000 signing bonus. This young man, a caring person, wants to do something for his old neighborhood. It is sinking into greater physical disrepair, and the kids growing up there are sliding into a life of despair. He knows that a first-class basketball court and sports program will get many of these potentially dead-end kids off the streets and on to the right track. He knows that once he can get them to compete in a healthy manner, he can hope that his program will expand to after-school tutoring and other beneficial programs.

Here is where Giving Back steps in: A young man such as this one has no idea whatsoever how to get from Point A to Point B. How much should it really cost? How do you find the right person to make it a reality? How much should this person be paid? Marc explained that there are many people who already do this, but take an unreasonable, even outrageous, percentage of the Tzedakah money as their a fee. As a result, the basketball star's $500,000 becomes a mere $50,000 worth of benefit for the kids. Marc and Giving Back have changed all of that. His concern is to share the vision of the basketball star, to fine-tune the actual project, and to bring it to fruition for a cost befitting someone whose ultimate concern is First Class Tzedakah and Tikun Olam with integrity.

...and Yet

Every day, well-intended, but misplaced, Tzedakah is happening. And it is being done by people with sums ranging from $1.00 to a gazillion dollars to donate to Tzedakah. And most of the donors are good-hearted, caring, and well-meaning people. It is still being done every day, by people (most of them good-hearted, caring, well-meaning people), who, by doing so, may unwittingly be depriving more suitable Mitzvah heroes or organizations from receiving critically-needed Tzedakah money for their own Tikun Olam work.

It is still being done every day by people — most of them good-hearted, caring, and well-meaning — but who should know better and could know better with just a little bit of effort on their part.

...and Yet

As this chapter, as well as others in this guide indicate, the situation can change.

What needs to be learned, can be partially learned alone, and the rest studied with the appropriate Tzedakah advisor. This advisor can provide direction that builds on a combination of the giver's own personality and wishes and the needs that most demand attention.

Doing Tzedakah better is not the same as asking people whose organic learning disability prevents them from doing better in math at school. Nor is it analogous to asking the most uncoordinated people to train for an Olympic gymnastics event. The skills, techniques, and ability to ask the right questions needed to do Tzedakah better are neither arcane nor hocus-pocus. Look around you, activate every part of your brain, and you will know which questions to ask. As stated above, the material to be learned is all "learnable", no matter where your starting point may be.

In Conclusion, Back to the Jewish Sources

The words of D'varim 30:11-14, which refers to God's teaching in general, would certainly apply to Tzedakah:

לא-נפלאת הוא ממך ולא-רחקה הוא
לא בשמים הוא
לאמר מי יעלה-לנו השמימה ויקחה לנו
וישמענו אתה ונעשנה
ולא-מעבר לים הוא
לאמר מי יעבר-לנו אל-עבר הים
ויקחה לנו וישמענו אתה ונעשנה
כי-קרוב אליך הדבר מאד
בפיך ובלבבך לעשתו

I paraphrase and interpret the translation:

> …it is not so awesome that you cannot grasp it, nor overwhelmingly far away from you.
> It is not in the Heavens that you should say, "Who can go up there, bring it down, and explain it to us so we can do it."
> It is not beyond the sea that you should say, "Who will cross this vast expanse, get it, and explain it to us so we can do it. "
> Ever–so–much to the contrary — it is incredibly close to you, already in your mouth when you express your desire to do Tzedakah and in your good and generous being to do."

Reasons for Giving

Pick a Tzedakah that you gave to or plan to give to.

Before giving, what do you think you should know about that Tzedakah fund?

When Is a Good Time to Give?

Make a list of 10 times that you think are "good times" to give Tzedakah:

1. *Friday evening before lighting Shabbat Candles*

2

3

4

5

6

7

8

9

10

Here's a few more. How many did you have on your list? How many can you add?

In the space before each answer, fill in 1, 2, 3 or 4 to indicate how often you would have the opportunity to give Tzedakah at the given time.
       1) hourly, (2) daily, (3) weekly, (4) monthly, or any combination of 1-4, or all of them

_____ Before lighting the candles for Shabbat and holidays

_____ Long enough before Shabbat or holidays to make certain others have been provided for so that they, too, can also enjoy Shabbat or the holiday

_____ When you arrive in Israel and throughout your time in Israel

_____ On יום העצמאות-Yom HaAtzma'ut, Israel Independence Day (the 5th of the Hebrew month of Iyyar)

_____ On יום הזכרון-Yom Hazikaron, The Day of Remembrance for fallen Israeli soldiers (the 4th of Iyyar)

_____ On יום ירושלים-Yom Yerushalayim The Anniversary of the Reunification of Jerusalem, June 1967 (the 28th of Iyyar)

_____ On יום הזכרון לשואה ולגבורה-Yom HaZikaron LaShoah VeLaGevura, Remembrance Day for Victims of the Shoah-Holocaust, and Resistance During the Shoah (the 27th of Nissan)

Here's a few more....

_____ Whenever you feel like it

_____ Whenever you don't feel like it, but you know that it is a Mitzvah

_____ Whenever you don't feel like it, but you have learned about a serious need

_____ Whenever you feel particularly happy

_____ Whenever you feel particularly sad, down, lonely, or depressed

_____ When you have made a serious promise that if X happens, you will donate Y dollars to Tzedakah.

In the classic Jewish legal sense of the term, a "נדר-neder, vow" is a formal verbal declaration. Jewish texts as far back as Biblical times describe the proper procedures for fulfilling the vow. At certain times in your life, you may make an "If this…, then this…" kind of promise in a most serious frame of mind. While this may not be exactly the same as a neder-vow, your intense sincerity was and is of great importance to you. Completing the process, i.e., donating to Tzedakah, can be a very fulfilling Life-experience.

_____ During a week-day minyan

_____ On the occasion of a Brit Milah (Bris), baby naming, Bar or Bat Mitzvah, Wedding, and other Jewish or secular joyous life-cycle event — anyone's

_____ When you or someone else — God forbid — is hospitalized, has a serious illness, or has received word of a troubling medical diagnosis

_____ When you or someone else has recovered from illness

_____ On a relative's or friend's yahrtzeit

_____ When you learn that a friend's relative has died

_____ On the occasion of a friend's becoming a Jew-by-choice

_____ Birthdays and anniversaries – anyone's

_____ When you hang a Mezuzzah on the doorposts of your house or apartment

_____ When you get a gift of money, receive a grant, or inherit money

_____ When you purchase something for yourself that will bring you happiness or comfort, or will serve as a useful tool or instrument either for your work or for your Tikun Olam work

_____ When you purchase a knickknack or tchatchka that is just for fun or just because you like it, or it fulfills your childhood fantasies — even if it looks weird or ruins the aesthetics of your kitchen or living room

_____ When you get hired for the job you always wanted

And here's a few more...

_____ When you get into your first choice college

_____ When you get an "A" on a tough exam

_____ Whenever you don't feel any specific high or low moment in your life

_____ Whenever you feel things have become too humdrum and routine

_____ Whenever you need to or really need to — for your own personal reasons

_____ When a family member gives birth

_____ When you get your Driver's Licence

_____ When you get your scores back on the SAT's

_____ When you are elected to a USY or school officer position

_____ When you pack for college and you add a Tzedakah box in your suitcase

_____ For no particular reason at all

_____ For good reason, but none that you can consciously think of

_____ All the time

_____ Whenever...

Now can you think of any others to add?

1

2

3

4

5

6

7

8

9

10

Time and Money

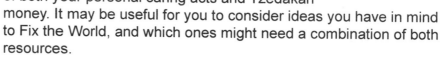

Doing Tikun Olam often requires a combination of both your personal caring acts and Tzedakah money. It may be useful for you to consider ideas you have in mind to Fix the World, and which ones might need a combination of both resources.

1. **List projects you have in mind, which need both personal time commitment and Tzedakah money:**

TIKUN OLAM PROJECT	TIME	MONEY

2. **Are you able to cover the entire cost of any of the projects listed using your own Tzedakah money?**

   Circle your answer: YES   NO

3. **If not, where would you look for additional funds to do these projects?**

How Does Jewish Tradition Define "Wealth"?

תנו רבנן: איזהו עשיר
כל שיש לו נחת רוח בעשרו דברי רבי מאיר
רבי טרפון אומר: כל שיש לו מאה כרמים ומאה שדות
ומאה עבדים שעובדין בהן
רבי עקיבא אומר: כל שיש לו אשה נאה במעשים
רבי יוסי אומר: כל שיש לו בית הכסא סמוך לשולחנו

Our Rabbis taught: Who is truly wealthy?
"Whoever gets satisfaction from his or her wealth, and feels at ease with it," — the words of Rabbi Meir.
Rabbi Tarfon says, "Whoever has 100 vineyards and 100 fields and 100 workers working in them."
Rabbi Akiva says, "Whoever has a spouse whose deeds are pleasant and pleasing."
Rabbi Yossi says, "Whoever has a bathroom near his or her dining room table."

(Talmud Shabbat 25b)

All four answers have merit.

Rabbi Meir's answer is fairly self-explanatory. He is saying, "What good is having so much if it doesn't give you deep contentment?" The Hebrew term "נחת רוח-nachat ruach" actually means your "spirit is at rest, at peace with itself".

Rabbi Tarfon's answer seems too simplistic. In modern terms, the wealthy Rabbi Tarfon appears to answer, "Rich — someone with $4,000,000 in liquid assets, 20,000 shares of rock-solid stocks in your portfolio, a six-bedroom penthouse on the Upper East Side of New York, another in Palm Springs for the Winter, and a mansion on Dor Dor VeDorshav Street in Jerusalem." However, I am sure Rabbi Tarfon had more in mind when he gave his answer. I have studied this passage with many of my audiences, and they have offered several fine interpretations. The one I like the most is that Rabbi Tarfon feels rich because he can provide jobs for 100 people. Nevertheless, on its most straightforward level, his answer is the one you most expect to hear.

Rabbi Akiva's answer makes sense — to be blessed with an intimate partner whose salient characteristics are Menschlichkeit and involvement in Tikun Olam.

My personal favorite, though, is Rabbi Yossi's. I think Rabbi Yossi is reacting to Rabbi Meir's and Rabbi Akiva's lofty responses. To Rabbi Yossi, you can have all the beauty and lyricism of what the other Rabbis taught, but for most people, taking care of the most fundamental matters of daily life is what really makes you wealthy.

How Much Are You Supposed to Give?

שיעור נתינתה: אם ידו משגת יתן כפי צורך העניים

ואם אין ידו משגת כל כך

יתן עד חומש נכסיו מצוה מן המובחר

ואחד מעשרה מדה בינונית פחות מכאן עין רעה...

הגה ואל יבזבז אדם יותר מחומש שלא יצטרך לבריות

The amount one should give to Tzedakah:
If one can afford it, enough to respond to all of the needs of the poor people.
But if one cannot afford that much,
then one should give up to a fifth of one's possessions —
which is doing the Mitzvah in an exceptional fashion —
one tenth is an average percentage,
and less is considered "poor eyesight" [i.e., giving less than needed because you may not have recognized how great the needs are]....
and one should not give away more than 20%,
lest he or she ultimately becomes dependent on others.

(Shulchan Aruch, Yoreh De'ah 249:1)

It Is All Right to Be Wealthy

Judaism does not set an upper limit to how much money a person should have. There is no prohibition against being wealthy. Certainly our tradition speaks out against people who are overly self-indulgent, but — in and of itself — there is nothing wrong with being a Rothschild, or one, two, or ten levels below "Rothschildkeit." As mentioned elsewhere in this book, the Jewish justification was expressed by someone whose father had said, "If you are going to live large, give large." In fact, in the practical world of fundraising, the different levels of wealth come into serious play. A mere millionaire may not be able to sway a multi-millionaire to give to a worthy Tzedakah project. Often, only a multi-millionaire soliciting another multi-millionaire can do it. "Big Money" works differently than "Small Money" in the Tzedakah sphere, just as it does in the "regular world". For example, to purchase and build a new Jewish camp such as Ramah Darom, the founders needed a large base of Big Tzedakah Money. Nickels and dimes usually aren't capable of doing that type of Tikun Olam. On several occasions, smaller donations multiplied by the thousands or millions have created the giant programs, but the general rule is you have to start with guarantees of hundreds of thousands or millions of dollars.

Consider big and small money in daily life: If you are buying a house, you won't usually quibble over $100 here or there. On the other hand, if you are in the supermarket and you notice that the price of Anjou pears has jumped 50¢ a pound in the last week, you may not buy them. So, too with Tzedakah money: For some people, it's all the same whether they give $2 million or $3 million for a worthy Tikun Olam program. For others, the quarter they donate on a given occasion according to that moment's available Tzedakah money is equally defined as "Tzedakah". Both the huge sums and the (mis-labeled) "small" money make a difference.

It Is NOT All Right to Impoverish Yourself Doing Tzedakah

Throughout the discussion in the previous two paragraphs, it should be clear that there is no Jewish ideal of self-impoverishment. Giving away all of your money and your possessions to do Tzedakah for others is not Jewish. In fact, in his classic Mishneh Torah law code, Maimonides states it with these stark words:

...ואין זו חסידות אלא שטות
שהרי הוא מאבד כל ממונו ויצטרך לבריות...
ובזה וכיוצא בו אמרו חכמים חסיד שוטה מכלל מבלי עולם

> ...this is not righteousness, but rather foolishness. Giving away all one's money causes that person to be in need of others....this is one of the situations the sages referred to when they taught, "A foolish righteous person is among those who 'wear the world out.'"
>
> (Hilchot Arachin Va'Charamin 8:13)

By "wear the world out", Maimonides means — that person becomes an additional drain on available resources. This is a setback to Tikun Olam, not a step forward. And that is why the rule is "One should not give away more than 20%".

Fixing Everything That Is Wrong in the Entire World

Now for the hard part — the opening lines of the Jewish law states:
The amount one should give to Tzedakah:
If one can afford it, enough to answer all the needs of the poor people.
But if one cannot afford that much, then...

Two comments:
1. This Jewish law can be traced back to Talmudic times, with sources going even further back to the Torah. In the Biblical and Talmudic mind, "all the needs of the poor people" meant a considerably smaller frame of reference than in today's world: your neighborhood, your village, your town, possibly your small city. It would be inconceivable to even the greatest Tzaddik in the Bible or Talmud that people could be connected by such technology as simple (to us in the 21st century) as a telephone, let alone a fax machine, radio, TV, and now e-mail and the internet. For us, "next door" is absolutely anywhere in the world. No one person could possibly satisfy "all the needs of the poor people" today.

And yet —

2. The opening line of the הלכה-Halachah, Jewish law remains valid. On first reading, you might react and say that this kind of thinking might be psychologically crushing. You do your part in Tikun Olam, and yet, you always know that there is a Big Wide World of other needs out there left to be done. You might become paralyzed by a feeling of guilt, inadequacy, or even utter helplessness, or you might increase your activities to the point of burn-out.

I understand the opening statement differently. I think what the Shulchan Aruch (and the Tanakh and Talmud before that) is teaching us is that total Tikun Olam is ultimately doable. There exists an incredible sum-total of needs; I don't dispute that fact. But, combined with working for systemic change, each person doing individual, personalized Tzedakah joins every other person doing the same. This yields a similarly huge sum-total of Tikun Olam. The outcome can be a world-in-repair. When considered in this light, the opening lines of the text — "Enough to respond to all of the needs of the poor people" — express an extremely positive approach to Tzedakah. I believe that they are an optimistic, energizing force for all who would wish to make the world a better, more Menschlich place for everyone.

The Jewish Percentage and Procedure

אַ֣ךְ כָּל־חֵ֡רֶם אֲשֶׁ֣ר יַחֲרִם֩ אִ֨ישׁ לַֽיה"וָ֜ה מִכָּל־אֲשֶׁר־ל֗וֹ
מֵאָדָ֤ם וּבְהֵמָה֙ וּמִשְּׂדֵ֣ה אֲחֻזָּת֔וֹ לֹ֥א יִמָּכֵ֖ר וְלֹ֣א יִגָּאֵ֑ל כָּל־חֵ֕רֶם ק"דֶשׁ־קָֽדָשִׁ֥ים
ה֖וּא לַֽיהוָֽה:

However no devoted thing, that a person shall devote to God of all that he has, both of man and beast, and of the field of his possession, shall be sold or redeemed; every devoted thing is most holy to God.

(Vayikra 27:28)

Basing his ruling on Tanakh text above and centuries-old traditions, Maimonides states that 10-20% is the appropriate amount to give to Tzedakah. Several comments will expand on his ruling:

1) According to most Jewish legal authorities, these percentages are to be calculated after taxes.

2) There are a few exceptions to the 20% upper limit, among them:
   A. If you are wealthy and there is no danger of your becoming dependent on others to meet your basic needs.
   B. You are permitted to give away more than 20% in a last will and testament.
   C. Securing the release of people in captivity. The assumption is that they are always in imminent danger of being killed. Sadly, the numerous savage murders of hostages in the Iraq War prove this point.

Reviewing the paragraphs above, it is clear that Jewish tradition affords you a range of possibilities. Within the specific range of percentages, you are afforded a certain flexibility and latitude to express your individualism and creativity.

One final comment to those who claim that they are neither creative nor talented: You may consider yourself a failure at piano or pottery-making, tone-deaf or athletically unfit for any sport other than checkers. Nevertheless, I assure you that there is every reason to believe that you will find yourself capable of true excellence, incredible creativity, and great distinction in your Tzedakah efforts.

What Can You Do If Your Money Is Limited?

Your personal financial situation may range from being nearly-Bill Gates-rich, to very comfortable, to modest, to "just getting by". Even if you are doing well, there may be things that happen that cause your actual money to shrink to levels which may cause you to think, "I need to cut back on my Tzedakah giving." That may be a natural tendency, but three Jewish texts address this issue and offer important insights for limited-income or fixed-income individuals, couples, and families.

Giving Money Away Incurs No Personal Loss

לעולם אין אדם מעני מן הצדקה
ואין דבר רע ולא היזק נגלל בשביל הצדקה
שנאמר והיה מעשה הצדקה שלום

No one ever becomes poor from doing Tzedakah,
nor does anything bad/ horrible/ unpleasant nor damaging result
from Tzedakah,
as the verse states, "and the end result of Tzedakah will be שלום-Shalom."
(Maimonides, Mishneh Torah, Matnot Ani'im, Laws of Gifts to Poor People, 10:2,
based upon Isaiah 32:17)

At first glance, this text sounds merely like a nice, comforting theme for a sermon. The Rabbis, however, were very practical-minded people, and they meant the words to be taken more seriously than simple sermonics. They had a deep understanding of day-to-day human existence.

The Rabbis were anything but naïve. They were constantly and passionately discussing why bad things happen to good people. I don't know just how much they believed a generous person's Tzedakah may protect them from the venom of a snakebite, but they clearly understood that Tikun Olam people would be protected from other potentially lethal forms of injury. They believed that Tzedakah could diminish the damaging force of insecurity, fear, and anxiety. That is why they used the term "דבר רע-davar ra". "רע-ra" has a range of meaning which includes everything from "not good" to "toxic" to "lethal" to "catastrophic".

Another text, mentioned earlier in this guide (Jerusalem Talmud [Venice Edition], Terumot 8:10) focuses specifically on the realities of money and how much it affects daily life:

כל האיברים תלוין בלב והלב תלוי בכיס
Every part of the human body depends on the heart,
But the heart depends on the pocket.

In the quote from Maimonides' stated above, the intent is that giving Tzedakah "enriches" your life, and that, if you are a giver, you will always feel at home in Life. You will never be impoverished by loneliness or fear of abandonment…because you are always connected to other people because of your acts of Tzedakah. Therefore, on an even more practical level, Maimonides and the Talmudic Rabbis also meant that giving your Tzedakah money strengthens your local, even global, society, people function better, the social order works more smoothly, and, as a result, you would not need to spend as much of your own money to live your own life as "normally" as before. You have made the world better, and while this is philosophically invaluable, in real dollars and cents, it means day-to-day living costs less.

To illustrate: Suppose you donate to a scholarship fund for at-risk kids. As a result, six more potentially dysfunctional children whose needs would have cost a fortune for therapy and care will (1) continue their education, (2) go to summer camp, (3) get into a job training program, and (4) become accomplished business people (hi-tech/physicians/chefs). They, in turn, donate their portion of Tzedakah back into the Great Pool of Tzedakah money, and everyone benefits.

Another illustration: Suppose you contribute some of your Tzedakah money to Independent Transportation Network (ITN) founded by Kathy Freund in Portland, Maine. Originally established in her local community, it continues to expand to many other cities in the United States. (www.itnamerica.org) ITN provides a heavily-discounted, personal transportation service for individuals no longer able to drive. Your elderly aunt and uncle no longer drive, cannot take public transportation for a variety of reasons, and do not have enough money for cab fares for their normal needs. Perhaps you used to send them $100 a month to help out. Now, you don't have to subsidize this particular need, because of Kathy's transportation network. Multiply that system of interconnections by thousands of other possibilities. Now Maimonides' and the Rabbis' statements make much more practical sense.

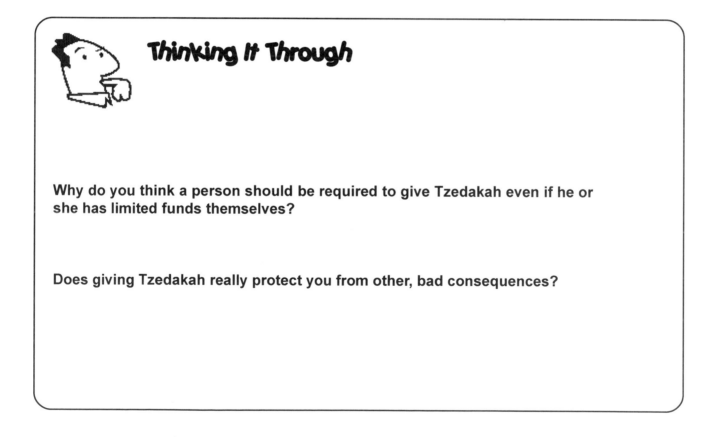

Thinking It Through

Why do you think a person should be required to give Tzedakah even if he or she has limited funds themselves?

Does giving Tzedakah really protect you from other, bad consequences?

Why Poor People are Expected to Give Tzedakah

אמר מר זוטרא אפילו עני המתפרנס מן הצדקה יעשה צדקה

Mar Zutra said:

Even a poor person who is supported by Tzedakah must give Tzedakah.

(Talmud Gittin 7b)

There are many reasons why Judaism expects poor people to give. The "high" reason is that if you take away a person's self-definition as a giver, you have taken away his or her self-dignity. This is an incredibly serious offense. My teacher, Rabbi Bradley Shavit Artson, says beautifully, "Tzedakah is not about giving; Tzedakah is about being." Being a Tzedakah-giver defines who you are as a person and as a Jew. To tell anyone that she or he is too poor to give is, in a way, tantamount to taking away her or his very existence.

Other reasons why poor people have to give include: (1) the poor person's actual dollars are needed in the overall pool of available Tzedakah funds, (2) the poor person knows how hard it is to live in serious financial difficulty and, therefore, may know better where to give Tzedakah money, and (3) with more money in the general pool available, better services will be provided by Mitzvah heroes and their Tikun Olam programs to improve the poor person's life.

Not Poor, But Not Wealthy or Even "Comfortable"

דרש רב עוירא זימנין א"ל משמיה דרב אמי
וזמנין אמר לה משמיה דרב אסי...
אם רואה אדם שמזונותיו מצומצמין
יעשה מהן צדקה וכ"ש כשהן מרובין

Rabbi Avira taught —
sometimes in the name of Rabbi Ammi
and sometimes in the name of Rabbi Assi:...
If a person sees that his or her [financial] resources are limited,
he or she should use them for Tzedakah,
and so much the more so when he or she has great [financial] resources.

(Talmud Gittin 7a)

Reasons for giving when your income is limited are similar to those listed in the previous section, with, perhaps, one important addition: The idea of "limited income" may vary much more in your mind than what it means to actually be poor. "Limited income" calls for an examination and re-examination of what you consider necessities for living a decent life, and what are only luxuries you can live without.

Rich, comfortable, living on a tight budget, or just "getting by", studies show that, while there may be trends, there is no absolute pattern to giving. Statistics often show that, in general, people in lower income brackets are better givers, but, with or without statistics and studies, your concern is your own pattern and extent of giving. While there certainly are generous wealthy and superwealthy people, there are, as well, some very wealthy individuals who are not particularly philanthropic. There are also people with limited income who are penny-pinchers, and still others who give with a hand always open to others. Every type of giver or non-giver exists in every income bracket. As stated above, though, your personal concern is your own giving. You will evaluate what you have, what you don't have, what you need, what you don't really need, and what others need, and then you will decide — with guidance from Jewish thought and practice — where to give accordingly.

Tzedakah Wishlists

What Is a Tzedakah Program's "Wish List" and Why Is It Sometimes Especially Important to Get a "Wish List" Before You Donate?

By Way of Introduction, Two Kinds of Wish Lists

In actuality there are two kinds of wish lists. One is a catalogue of actual needs, and the other is a list of needs plus an "add-on". By an "add-on", I mean, the amount you would contribute for the "Kavod", the honor of being recognized publicly for your donation. This includes items such as having the reading room in a library named for you. The actual cost may be $200,000, but your expected donation is $500,000, because the room will always be known as the Porath Reading Room. This chapter deals with only the former type of wish list, namely, actual costs of the item.

Why There Are Wish Lists

No matter how recently a brochure, annual report, or website has been updated, there are often many late-breaking needs for any Mitzvah hero or Tzedakah organization. Time and again, needs arise even a few hours before you contact the Mitzvah hero or organization. The "wish list" focuses on what is needed right at that moment. Usually, the wish list is a catalogue of short-term needs, including items that may be immediately solvable by your personal donation. To name a few: The delivery truck for a food recycling operation may desperately need new tires or insurance now, a shelter for victims of domestic violence may need to pay rent and utilities now, the price of gasoline has risen and operations are grinding to a halt because the Mitzvah hero can no longer afford to reach all of the people with whom she or he is working to restore them to good physical or mental health.

There are even situations where long-term needs have become a higher priority on the wish list. After months of discussion, you may be in touch just at the time when a Mitzvah hero or organization has decided to develop a new program because the demand for that kind of Tikun Olam has become so great. Of infinite possibilities, the following three examples should illustrate my point:

1. Someone appears as if "out of nowhere" who could be an ideal year-long assistant to help expand the program.

2. After a natural disaster, a dozen families that previously had manageable needs, now have to re-locate and begin a new life. They have been left with nothing but the clothing they wore when they were rescued. The demands for Tzedakah money may be enormous.

3. A recent wave of immigrants from Ethiopia has just arrived in Israel, and accommodating for their needs has placed greater demands on the organization that is working with them. Depending on the circumstances, the wish list for both short-term and long-term needs can be very long.

Why You Might Ask to See a Wish List

In addition, your personal reasons for asking for the wish list may include:

1. The Mitzvah hero's or organization's work is so extensive, you would like to focus on a specific aspect of the Tikun Olam work so that your donation will not be "swallowed up" in the overall program.
2. You like to feel that you have totally eliminated at least one of the Mitzvah heroes' or organizations' needs. (They like to hear words like, "I can do that" or "Solved! Next...")
3. You want to have as great an impact on their Tikun Olam work as possible.

Thinking It Through

What kind of research would you do to determine where to spend your Tzedakah money?

The following suggestions may be of use as you do your research on this aspect of your Tzedakah work:

1. Once you have located Mitzvah heroes or Tikun Olam programs that appeal to you, contact them directly.
2. Make certain to speak to the person who is most knowledgeable about the real needs and who is best able to tell you all the details.
3. Ask if your donation is needed more for discretionary use, for wish list items, or a combination of both.
4. If the person says that wish list items are critical, give him or her a general range of how much Tzedakah money you are considering donating to the Tikun Olam work. Even if you are thinking of giving "only" $18 or $25, there is no need to be embarrassed. You have been open with them, and you may find something on a wish list that fits your Tzedakah giving so well, you will decide to donate more than you had originally intended. This happens frequently with wish lists.
5. If something on the wish list particularly appeals to you, you may want to divide your contribution so that a portion helps to cover the overall work and another portion is dedicated to something on the wish list.
6. You will often discover that you are so taken by the wish list, you may decide to contribute 100% of what you had already decided to donate plus additional Tzedakah money for the items on the wish list. This, too, happens frequently.

A concluding thought:

Working with wish lists may well fit your own pattern of Tzedakah. After more than 30 years of experience with my own Ziv Tzedakah Fund, I have found that this aspect of giving makes a huge difference and is worth your serious consideration.

How Can You Make the Most of Your Tzedakah Money?

"Bang for the Buck" in Regular Life

In "regular" life you stretch your money all the time:

> You look for department store sales.
> You compare prices before buying insurance, a computer, or a car.
> You have finally reached the age when you get senior citizen discounts at the movies and on trains and planes.
> You use coupons from newspapers, magazines, and flyers that come in the mail.
> You love "twofers" — two tickets to a play for the price of one.
> You surf the internet for the lowest possible airfares.
> Colloquially, you call this "getting more bang for the buck", and rarely would you opt for a higher price if you could stretch your money by any reasonable means.

Get the Bang for Your Tzedakah Buck

Can you think of ways to stretch your Tzedakah dollar? Where do you think you would get the most "bang for your buck?"
Make a list of all the ways you can think of to stretch your Tzedakah dollars.

1.

2.

3.

4.

5.

6.

7.

8.

9.

10.

"Bang for the Tzedakah Buck"

You can stretch your Tzedakah money to accomplish more Tikun Olam, just as you do in "regular" life. In most cases this is known as "leveraging your Tzedakah money".

Here are just a few examples:

1. Interest-free loan societies: A particularly beautiful way to leverage your Tzedakah money is to support a Jewish interest-free loan society. In Hebrew it is called a גמ"ח-Gemach, an abbreviation for "גמילות חסד-Gemillut Chessed", an act of caring lovingkindness. The Jewish practice of offering interest-free loans extends back millennia to Biblical times. The beauty of it is that the money continues to re-circulate. Once loans begin to be repaid, that money goes right back out for other loans. And most Gemachs have a default rate of less than three or four percent. To give you a sense of the "rate of return" on an interest-free loan investment, Ziv Tzedakah Fund's cumulative donations to the Israel Free Loan Association over approximately 15 years totaled $51,484. As of April, 2006, this sum had generated $284,040 in the form of 237 loans — a return of 552%! Surf the website of the International Association of Hebrew Free Loans (IAHFL) at www.freeloan.org to learn more about interest-free loans.

2. Matching Funds: Once you have found Mitzvah heroes or Tzedakah programs you want to support, you may find that they have been offered a matching grant. Every dollar you give will be matched one-for-one, two-for-one, or even more by some other donor. A striking example is this: In the aftermath of the devastation of Hurricane Katrina, one individual lined up several people who committed to match donations. By the time he had finished creating his Tzedakah consortium, he had assembled an eight-to-one arrangement. This meant that for every $100 you donated, it actually amounted to $900 for Katrina relief.

3. Their expertise: Through your research, you may discover Mitzvah heroes who are experts at obtaining discounts for goods and services they need in their Mitzvah work. Because what they are doing is so right and so good, others may want to join them by offering everything at cost or for free. Your Mitzvah money will stretch nicely if you know that a Mitzvah hero who needs to buy a van has done her or his research and can purchase it at cost.

4. Built into the Mitzvah hero's project: Similarly, if a Mitzvah hero retrieves food from hotels, restaurants, and other food establishments and provides the food for people in need, your donation of $100 may equal as much as, or more than, 10 times the store-purchased value. For instance, you may decide to pay $300 to rent a bus to bring volunteers to an orchard to glean the fruit. A day's gleaning could easily yield $5,000-$10,000 worth of clementines, onions, or strawberries for food banks and soup kitchens.

5. Mitzvah hero partnerships: You may also find a Mitzvah hero such as Joseph Gitler and his Table to Table program in Israel. (www.tabletotable.org.il) He is a supreme expert at "partnering" — working with already-established programs. He finds trustworthy local programs that provide food to people in need. His part, then, in providing for hungry people is simply to retrieve the food and get it from Point Alef to Point Bet, as with the fruit gleaning mentioned in #4. This saves tremendously on overhead costs. (In the United States, Ken Horne's Society of St. Andrew/The Potato Project is doing similarly astonishing work. www.endhunger.org)

6. Your own initiative: This, too, could play a vital role in stretching your Tzedakah money. For example, winter is about to hit your hometown of Minneapolis. You take it upon yourself to approach the owner or manager of a large clothing store and to say that you would like to buy sweaters for people in need. It may happen that the owner or manager will give you a discount, donate the sweaters, or give you both the discount and also add several sweaters (and sweatshirts, gloves, hats, and long underwear) as a donation from the store. Frequently, owners and managers can't help in this way because of too many similar requests, a slowdown in the economy, or similar reasons, but you should always feel that you are entitled to ask. It isn't necessary that you have a personal connection to the store, e.g., the owner is your old sorority sister from college. Because you are on a Mitzvah mission, you may feel moved to just do it "cold", and since you are not asking for yourself, you will almost always get a sympathetic response whether or not you actually get a discount or 100% donated items.

7. At work: Many corporate holiday parties have been cancelled or seriously downgraded to a less elaborate bash because one individual suggested it to the boss. (You could be that individual.) The money saved is then donated to an appropriate Tikun Olam project. And more — many employees may feel moved to donate to the designated program, and your own donation will now represent substantially more dollar-benefit to the recipients.

8. Testimonial dinners: You may suggest to an organization that it change its annual dinner to a dessert reception. While it is true that these gatherings powerfully publicize the good work, and the "electricity" in the room reinforces the attendees' commitment, many groups could accomplish the same with a dessert reception. The evening's expense will be greatly reduced, and a greater percentage of what everyone pays to attend the event will then go to the Tzedakah program's real work — doing Tikun Olam.

Ray Buchanan's Incredible Feat of Leveraging

The best example of Tzedakah leveraging I learned of recently comes from Ray Buchanan, founder of Stop Hunger Now (SHN, www.stophungernow.org), an international relief organization providing food, medicines, and other critical items in several countries throughout the world. I have known Ray for many years, and Stop Hunger Now is always my first choice whenever a Tikun Olam situation arises that falls within his realm of expertise. Responding to a question about an astonishing leveraging effort he made, this is what he reported:

> Recently, SHN was offered $18,000,000 of food if we could take care of all the shipping, transportation and admin costs...which amounted to $75,000. Almost at the same time, we were given the opportunity to provide $650,000 worth of critically needed medicines for Northern Uganda and Southern Sudan...if we could cover a $12,000 distribution cost....We were able to do both...because of the generosity and faithfulness of our friends and supporters. Working together allowed us to leverage $87,000 into almost $19,000,000 worth of life-saving food and medicine.

By simple division, Buchanan's leveraging yields a return of more than $214 in delivered Mitzvah goods for every $1 contributed to Stop Hunger Now. This is truly a staggering accomplishment, and while few Mitzvah heroes and Tzedakah programs can achieve this exceptional degree of successful leveraging and partnering, the principle remains the same: By using your researching talents and common sense, your Tzedakah can often make things happen far beyond your imagining.

The "And Yet"

And yet, all the good intentions, exquisite sensitivity and desire to do good, and the massive sympathy of others would not have been enough if Ray did not have the actual $87,000 of Tzedakah he needed when he set out to provide so much good for so many people. When I teach, I usually tell my students, "You can't do $10 worth of Tikun Olam with only $9 in Tzedakah money, or $100 worth of Tikun Olam with only $90, or $1,000 worth with only $900." Buchanan, and others teach us that you can, indeed, do millions of dollars worth of Tikun Olam with thousands of dollars. Now I add, "But you still need the thousands of dollars."

7 Questions Concerning Using Your Money For Tikun Olam

Complete the following:

1. Have you used the same amount of brain-and-heart power to make decisions about your Tzedakah money as you did when you thought about how to spend your personal money?

    Circle your answer:

    YES   NO

    If so, list some examples:

2. Have you studied the distinctly Jewish methods of giving Tzedakah and how they contrast with and compare to methods of giving in other religions and cultures?

    Circle your answer:

    YES   NO

    If so, list things you learned from your study:

3. Are your Tzedakah advisors as skilled and wise about where to give Tzedakah as your teachers, parents and friends?

    Circle your answer:

    YES   NO

    If yes, list your Tzedakah advisors and what impresses you about their advice?

4. Did you take into account that Tzedakah money often has more "buying power" than "regular money", i.e., that you can often change and save lives with less money than it takes to change the oil in your car?

    Circle your answer:

    YES   NO

    If so, give examples of "Tzedakah buying power" that particularly impressed you:

(Continued on Next Page)

5. Did you ever look at coins and dollar bills and think that — if properly donated — these really small sums of money could radically improve the lives of others?

Circle your answer:

YES   NO

If so, give examples.

6. If you have looked at coins and dollar bills this way — did you ever think that you would be getting such enjoyment-שׂמחה–from giving your money away?

Circle your answer:

YES   NO

If so, what words would you use to explain this unique feeling to others?

7. Did you ever imagine that, once you began to do Tikun Olam to this extent —changing and saving lives with money — that you would want to do more and more of it, even if it meant that you might have less money for your personal use?

Circle your answer:

YES   NO

> **Now, review your answers and write a paragraph articulating how you would describe your relationship to both kinds of money — money for your own use and Tzedakah money.**

Developing Tzedakah Priorities

Placing Priority

If you had to decide the best way to give tzedakah, could you?

There seem to be five essential axes around which people make decisions about priorities in Jewish philanthropy. For each pair of choices consider which you would rather give Tzedakah for and then circle that answer.

serve Jews		serve anyone
give food or meals	**or**	lobby to raise the minimum wage
help Jews in your city		help Jews in Israel
provide food, shelter, or medical care		provide education or preserve the earth
help people in North America		help people in the poorest countries

Write your own levels of giving tzedakah from the most selfless way to the most selfish way.

Most Selfless _____

_____

_____

_____

_____

Most Selfish _____

_____

_____

_____

What are the most important ways that you can give Tzedakah?

Maimonides' Ladder of Tzedakah
(in descending order)

Maimonides developed the following priority order for giving Tzedakah with the intention of preserving the dignity of the recipient. He recognized that a challenge exists for both the giver and the receiver and tried to make the process as easy as possible. Maimonides took the approach that it is better to give grudgingly rather than not at all, but makes it clear that the highest level of Tzedakah is when the recipients are given a skill to earn their own money and never have to ask for money again.

> **FYI:** Moses ben Maimon (1135-1204), a rabbinic authority of Spanish birth, codifier, philosopher, and royal physician, is known in Rabbinic literature as "Rambam" from the acronym Rabbi Moses Ben Maimon ("Maimonides" = "son of Maimon"). He spent ten years writing the *Mishneh Torah*, a codification of the Oral Law, from which he believed all Jews could systematically learn (in his words) the correct way to determine what was forbidden and permitted, as well as other laws of the Torah. The task of the *Mishneh Torah* was to present the results of Rambam's own study of the literature written by the Rabbis in talmudic times in such a way that everyone, and not only scholars, could understand what behaviors were required of them. The *Mishneh Torah* is divided into 14 books, each representing a distinct category of the Jewish legal system. The selection below is excerpted from the section of the *Mishneh Torah* entitled "Hilchot Matanot Aniyyim" – "Laws of Gifts fto Poor People" 10:7-14)

Maimonides Mix-Up

Look at the following items and put them in order from the best way to give Tzedakah (1) to the least desirable way to give Tzedakah (8). After you have done this exercise, then look at the next page to see how Maimonides ordered them.

_____ Giving Before One is Asked to Give

_____ Giving Less Than Appropriate, But Cheerfully

_____ Giving Anonymously (Neither You nor the Receiver Know the Other)/ Tzedakah Fund

_____ Giving to a Person Who Knows it Came From You, But You Do Not Know Him

_____ Giving a Person a Gift or Loan/ Finding a Job (So They Don't Have to Ask Anymore)

_____ Giving Reluctantly

_____ Giving to a Person Who Does Not Know it Came From You, But You Know Him

_____ Giving After One is Asked to Give

שמנה מעלות יש בצדקה זו למעלה מזו'

מעלה גדולה שאין למעלה ממנה זה המחזיק ביד ישראל שמך

ונותן לו מתנה או הלואה או עושה עמו שותפות או ממציא לו מלאכה

כדי לחזק את ידו עד שלא יצטרך לבריות לשאול'

ועל זה נאמר והחזקת בו גר ותושב וחי עמך

כלומר החזק בו עד שלא יפול ויצטרך.

ח פחות מזה הנותן צדקה לעניים ולא ידע למי נתן ולא ידע העני ממי לקח'

שהרי זו מצוה לשמה' כגון לשכת חשאים שהיתה במקדש'

שהיו הצדיקים נותנין בה בחשאי והעניים בני טובים מתפרנסין ממנה בחשאי'

וקרוב לזה הנותן לתוך קופה של צדקה'

ולא יתן אדם לתוך קופה של צדקה

אלא אם כן יודע שהממונה נאמן וחכם ויודע להנהיג כשורה כר' חנניה בן תרדיון.

ט פחות מזה שידע הנותן למי יתן ולא ידע העני ממי לקח'

כגון גדולי החכמים שהיו הולכין בסתר ומשליכין המעות בפתחי העניים'

וכזה ראוי לעשות ומעלה טובה היא אם אין הממונין בצדקה נוהגין כשורה.

י פחות מזה שידע העני ממי נטל ולא ידע הנותן'

כגון גדולי החכמים שהיו צוררים המעות בסדיניהן ומפשילין לאחוריהן

ובאין העניים ונוטלין כדי שלא יהיה להן בושה.

יא פחות מזה שיתן לו בידו קודם שישאל.

יב פחות מזה שיתן לו אחר שישאל.

יג פחות מזה שיתן לו פחות מן הראוי בסבר פנים יפות.

יד פחות מזה שיתן לו בעצב.

1. The highest degree is to strengthen the hand of a Jew who is poor, giving that person a gift or loan or becoming a partner or finding a job for that person, to strengthen the person's hand, so that the person will not need to ask for assistance from others...

2. A lesser degree, is one who gives Tzedakah to a poor person and is unaware of the recipient, who, in turn, is unaware of the giver. This is indeed a religious act achieved for its own sake. Of a similar character is one who contributes to a Tzedakah fund. One should not contribute to a Tzedakah fund unless he or she knows that the person in charge of the collections is trustworthy and wise and knows how to manage the money properly...

3. The [third], lesser, degree is when the giver knows the recipient, but the recipient does not know the giver. The great sages used to go secretly and cast the money into the doorway of poor people. Something like this should be done, it being a noble virtue, if the Tzedakah administrators are not behaving properly.

4. The [fourth], still lower, degree is when the recipient knows the giver, but the giver does not know the recipient. The great sages used to tie money in sheets which they threw behind their backs, and poor people would come and get it without being embarrassed.

5. The [fifth], still lower degree is when the giver puts the Tzedakah money into the hands of poor people without being solicited.

6. The [sixth], still lower degree is when he or she puts the money into the hands of a poor person after being solicited.

7. The [seventh], still lower degree is when he or she gives the poor person less than he or she should, but does so cheerfully.

8. The [eighth], still lower degree is when he or she gives the poor person grudgingly/with a feeling of pain/unhappily.

(Mishneh Torah, Laws of Gifts to Poor People, 10:7-14)

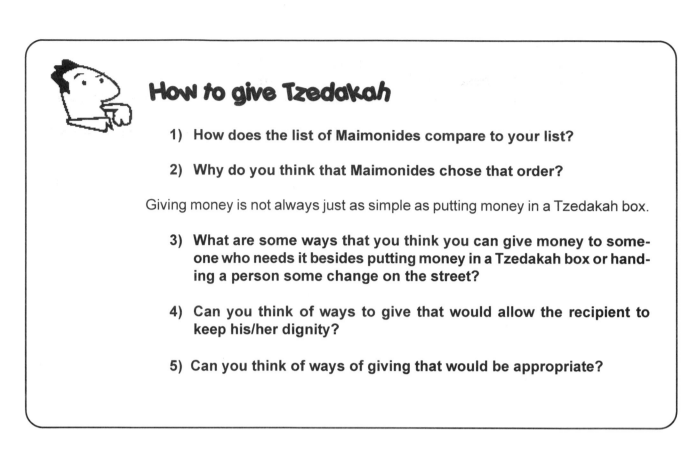

How to give Tzedakah

1) How does the list of Maimonides compare to your list?

2) Why do you think that Maimonides chose that order?

Giving money is not always just as simple as putting money in a Tzedakah box.

3) What are some ways that you think you can give money to someone who needs it besides putting money in a Tzedakah box or handing a person some change on the street?

4) Can you think of ways to give that would allow the recipient to keep his/her dignity?

5) Can you think of ways of giving that would be appropriate?

Maimonides Match-Up

Each of the following texts demonstrates a way of giving Tzedakah according to the Maimonides Ladder. Using what you have learned, try to match up the text with the correct ladder step. (Please note that not every step is represented!)

There were two chambers in the Temple, one of which was the Secret Chamber....
Menschlich people would secretly bring money to the Secret Chamber,
and poor people would secretly take from it for their livelihood.

(Mishna Shekalim 5:6)

Maimonides Level: _____

How much should one give to a poor person?
Whatever it is that the person might need.
How is this to be understood?
If the person is hungry, he or she should be fed.
If the person needs clothes, he or she should be provided with clothes.
If the person has no household furniture or utensils, furniture and utensils should

be provided....

And similarly to every individual according to what is needed:

A person who needs bread should be given bread;

Dough — the person should be given dough; a bed — the person should be given a bed;

A person who needs warm bread, should be given warm bread, cold bread — bold bread,

If the person needs to be spoonfed, then we must spoonfeed the person.

(Shulchan Aruch, Yoreh De'ah, 250:1)

Maimonides Level: _____

A Tanna taught: If he is a beggar who goes from door to door, we pay no attention to him. A certain man who used to beg from door to door came to Rav Papa (for money), but he ignored him. Rav Samma the son of Rav Yeva said to R. Papa, "If you do not pay attention to him, no one else will pay attention to him; is he then to die of hunger?" [R. Papa replied] "But has it not been taught, 'If he is a beggar who goes from door to door, we pay no attention to him'?" He replied, "We do not listen to his request for a large amount, but we do listen to his request for a small amount."

(Talmud Bava Batra 9a)

Maimonides Level: _____

Rabbi Abba said in the name of Rabbi Shimon bar Lakish: "One who lends (money) is greater than one who performs charity; and one who forms a partnership is greater than all."

(Talmud Shabbat 63a)

Maimonides Level: _____

[Rav. Hana b. Hanilai] had sixty bakers in his house day and night, baking for anyone who needed bread. He who always kept a hand in his pocket, thinking, "A poor person who was once financially stable may come along, and by the time I reach into my pocket to give, the person may feel humiliated."

(Talmud Berachot 58b)

Maimonides Level: _____

The Real-Life Story

Many years ago, my friend, Dr. Jay Masserman, told me a very moving story from his days as a resident. It is about The Human Touch, and bears re-telling in this volume.

An eminent physician is taking his students on morning rounds. Here and there he explains to his entourage some fine point of the art of healing, adding to their store of insight and knowledge so that when they assume their positions as Healers, they, too, will remonstrate the requisite skill and wisdom needed to ease suffering and pain. The professor's expertise impresses the interns and residents.

As they go from room to room, the professor and students encounter an older woman recently arrived as a "social admission". She is not desperately ill, but her complex of ailments makes it impossible for her neighbors and friends to take care of her. The professor sees that she is depressed, withdrawn. She refuses to eat. There is nothing here to be revealed in the way of book-knowledge; no advanced scholarship is needed.

The professor stops, and for twenty minutes feeds the woman.

She is capable of feeding herself, but she refuses to do so. So, with deliberate and gentle care, the teacher teaches a lesson in kindness. He does not do it as a demonstration to the students. No, he spoonfeeds this old woman because that is what the demands of the hour are. If, as a result of this long delay, the students will have missed some detail of graduate training, some fact concerning prescriptions or diagnosis, it matters little to the professor.

Human beings must be served with a touch of humanity.

Developing Guidelines For Giving

Utilizing your knowledge from the collecting and distributing experiences and from discussing texts from the Talmud, establish a list of guidelines which you consider to be the best ways to collect and distribute money for Tzedakah. When you have determined a number of guidelines, list them in priority order with number 1 as the most important and number 10 as the least important.

Collecting	Distributing
1	1
2	2
3	3
4	4
5	5
6	6
7	7
8	8
9	9
10	10

Why Does it Sometimes Feel So Difficult to Give Your Money Away?

אשרי משכיל אל דל

Happy is the person who is משכיל–Maskil in relation to the person in need.

(Psalm 41:2)

אמר ר' יונה אשרי נותן אל דל אין כת' כן
אלא אשרי משכיל אל דל הוי מסתכל בו היאך לזכות בו

Rabbi Yonah said,

"Happy is the person who gives to the person in need"
is not what the verse says, but rather,

"Happy is the one who is משכיל-Maskil in relation to the person in need,"
meaning,

"Look at the situation carefully,
and keep in mind how it is a privilege to do the Mitzvah through that person."

(Midrash Leviticus Rabba 34:1; Margoliot Edition 4:773)

Judaism considers giving Tzedakah a *privilege*. In the above passage, Rabbi Yonah wonders why Psalm 41 didn't use the verb "נתן-give". Why doesn't the verse simply state, "Happy is the person who gives to the person in need"? Instead, the word is "משכיל-Maskil", from the root "שכל". This is the same root in modern Hebrew and traditional Yiddish that gives us *seichel*, usually translated as "common sense". Centuries ago, though, it meant the entire range of your mental, spiritual, psychological, and emotional capabilities, including your intelligence, imagination, talents, and common sense. Rabbi Yonah stresses that all of these aspects of your personality should come into play when you create a relationship with a person in need with your Tzedakah money.

What is particularly interesting are the Rabbi's closing words, "היאך לזכות בו". "לזכות- lizkot", comes from the same Hebrew root as "זכות-privilege". Indeed, in that same chapter of the Midrash, a poor person says, "זכי בי"-Zaki Bi. Have the privilege of doing Tzedakah through me." Once again, the same Hebrew root is used. In the language of the Jews nearly 2,000 years ago, this was a natural way to say, "I need help, and I have chosen you to be the one to set things right."

It may not be easy to shift your Mitzvahs, Tzedakah, and Tikun Olam mindset to one of "privilege". Nevertheless, those who have succeeded in making the transition have told me that it feels as though a great weight has been lifted from their shoulders. Some have even described this insight as "revelatory", and that, as a result, their labors on behalf of others now give greater meaning to their lives.

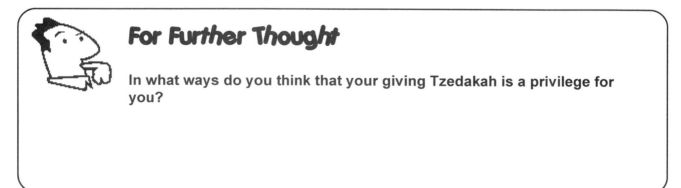

For Further Thought

In what ways do you think that your giving Tzedakah is a privilege for you?

How Important Is Your Attitude and Intent?

פחות מזה שיתן לו בעצב

A still lower level is giving בעצב-BeEtzev.

(Maimonides, Mishneh Torah,
Hilchot Matnot Ani'im, Laws of Gifts to Poor People, 10:14)

This is the eighth, the lowest, level in Maimonides' famous list of Tzedakah giving. The key word here is "בעצב". The root "עצב" can have many meanings including "sadness", "distress", "pain", and "labor" (including "labor pains"). The eighth level, therefore, means that the person is giving, but reluctantly, and is at great pains to donate. What is crucial to understand is that, even though giving grudgingly is at the bottom of the list, *it is still an act of Tzedakah*. **I cannot stress this point strongly enough.** The Jewish definition of Tzedakah is that you have taken some of your money and used it for the benefit of others. While it would be wonderful if everyone gave willingly and cheerfully, very *real* money is what is needed in the very *real* world of Tikun Olam.

This text supports my position on public school community service requirements. In most high schools in North America and all high schools in Israel, students are required to do a certain number of hours of community service in order to graduate. I think that this is one of the greatest ventures in the field of education...even if we arbitrarily estimate that 16% of the students do it only because it will look good on their college applications. I have no problem with that. Just consider the staggering number of lives that have been changed for the better since the service requirement was instituted in high schools. Give it a real number — say 100,000,000 lives. (I personally believe that that is a very conservative estimate.) If my Mitzvah math is correct that 16% of the students do their Tikun Olam for less-than-100% pure goodness, then this means that 16,000,000 people are living better as a result of the students' community service requirement. Breaking the accepted rules of fine writing, I state again, "16,000,000 people are living better as a result of the students' community service requirement!!!!!!"

I rest my case.

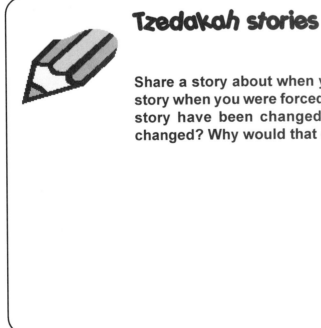

Tzedakah stories

Share a story about when you were happy to donate money. Then share a story when you were forced to donate money. Could anything in the second story have been changed to make you happy? What could have been changed? Why would that change have made you happy?

Should You Always Do Your Tzedakah Giving Anonymously?

Background:

Maimonides' Principles of Tzedakah and the Issue of Secret and Anonymous Giving

מעלה גדולה שאין למעלה ממנה זה המחזיק ביד ישראל שמך
ונותן לו מתנה או הלואה או עושה עמו שותפות או ממציא לו מלאכה
כדי לחזק את ידו עד שלא יצטרך לבריות לשאול...
פחות מזה הנותן צדקה לעניים ולא ידע למי נתן ולא ידע העני ממי לקח
שהרי זו מצוה לשמה...

The highest degree [of Tzedakah] is to strengthen the hand of a Jew who is poor, giving thatperson a gift, or a loan, or becoming a partner, or finding a job for that person — to strengthen the person's hand, so that the person can become self-supporting and will not have to be dependent on others....

One degree lower is a person who gives Tzedakah to poor people and is unaware of the recipients, who in turn are unaware of the giver. This is indeed a Mitzvah achieved for its own sake....

(Maimonides, Mishneh Torah,
Hilchot Matnot Ani'im, Laws of Gifts to Poor People, 10:7-8)

At my lectures, I frequently ask, "What is Maimonides' *highest* level of Tzedakah?" Quite often the answer given is, "When the recipient doesn't know the donor, and when the donor doesn't know the recipient." Reading the actual source, though, we see that they are really responding to Maimonides' second level. The highest level includes finding someone a job so she or he can become self-suffi-cient. In that situation, you have to know enough about the person, perhaps even conducting an interview, in order to provide the appropriate match for employment.

Three additional examples provide a broader understanding of Maimonides' highest level of Tzedakah. Each requires "non-anonymity". (However, your donation to these kinds of Tzedakah organizations preserves your own anonymous relationship to the actual recipient.)

1. Pa'amonim-פעמונים–is an organization in Israel that works specifically with a certain well-de-fined category of people who have fallen between the cracks of the government social service system. They are individuals and families who are definitely close to being able to re-establish their financial stability — provided they receive the proper guidance. Some of the issues Pa'amonim deals with are credit card debt, temporary or long-term job loss, unexpected illness and similar extraordinary circumstances. Pa'amonim could not do its work without knowing all the necessary details (including information in bank statements and similar documents) of the people with whom they are working. See www.paamonim.com for more details.

2. As their name indicates, Jewish free-loan societies offer interest-free loans. They also require certain knowledge about the borrower. (Free-loan societies are discussed at length in the chapter Should I Accept Tzedakah Money If I Need It?)

3. Millions of individuals and families have completely broken out of the cycle of poverty by receiving loans of as little as $50 or less. This kind of Tzedakah is known as "microloans", a

concept invented by a single individual, Muhammad Yunus. The worldwide microloan movement is one of the great Tzedakah stories of the modern age, and billions of dollars have been successfully invested in people's lives with astonishing results. The incredibly wise theory of microloans coupled with the most remarkably well thought out practical process of distribution can leave you stunned, sometimes breathless, and occasionally saying to yourself, "Why didn't someone think of this hundreds of years ago?" Visit the following two websites to get the full story: www.grameen-info.com and www.gfusa.org. Obviously, the process of extending microloans to the appropriate recipients requires that anonymity be suspended.

To review: On Maimonides' scale of Tzedakah, it is the second level that requires anonymity. Both anonymous and non-anonymous Mitzvahs have their place. It all depends on the situation at hand, and in some of your Tzedakah work, you may want to do both kinds of Tikun Olam.

On the Absolute Need to Talk About Your Tzedakah Work

There is an absolute need for you to talk about your Tzedakah work with others — family, friends, others exploring their own Tzedakah giving. Unfortunately, I believe that many people have taken Maimonides' 2nd level and extended it to mean that they should never tell anyone what they are doing with their Tzedakah money. Actually, there is an operative Jewish principle which supersedes the principle of secrecy — כדי לחנכו במצות –for the sake of Mitzvah education. This principle is mentioned in several different contexts in Talmudic literature and would most certainly apply to many areas of Tzedakah. In my opinion, there is a desperate need to share your Tzedakah knowledge and experience with others, so that they will not only be encouraged to do more of their own giving, but also so that they will have become more skilled at how they can give Tzedakah.

When you are telling about your own Tzedakah work, you should, of course, protect the anonymity of recipients. You will also need to decide whether or not to tell others how much you have given in each situation. But neither of these prevents you from telling others, "I have discovered these incredibly fine Mitzvah heroes (or Tzedakah organizations), have done all my due diligence and homework, checked them out 100%, and would like you to know more about them. And, as a result, I have given them some of my Tzedakah money to show that I believe in what they are doing." If you choose to do this, you will accomplish two things: (1) You may gain additional support for the people doing fine Tikun Olam, and (2) you may prevent others from misdirecting funds to either inefficient or unworthy individuals or organizations. However you do this — by personal conversation or by any other means at your disposal — you will be changing the direction of the trend that says, "What I do with my Tzedakah money is my own business."

When Secrecy and Anonymity Is a "Must"

You will encounter many situations where you want to absolutely keep your identity secret. A classic situation is when a relative, friend, or acquaintance is in need, and you want to offer financial support. Even beyond that circle of people, it could be anyone who might possibly know you and who would be embarrassed to find out that you had contributed. In that situation, your best option is a third party, such as a Tzedakah fund or Rabbi's discretionary fund, both of which can route the money to the recipient without any fear of your participation being discovered.

What About Plaques?

One extreme end of the scale is the joke about an institution's building that was made entirely out of donor's plaques. Not so far removed are places you have been where the walls are covered with names and categories of giving including "Angel", "President's Circle", "Builder", "Patron", and "Benefactor". Then there are institutions and organizations that restrict plaques to one small corner of the building. Finally, there are those that have no names whatsoever — not on the campus, the building, the program, not on a single plaque or certificate of recognition anywhere.

There is a similar scale of people's reactions to plaques and its related phenomenon, "naming opportunities" — from "none" to "as many as needed to bring in the money we need". You have your own view of what is in good taste and appropriate. More accurately, most likely you have a general opinion one way or another, but allow for specific exceptions. If you find this practice overdone, keep in mind that the plaque syndrome is not 100% about the ego needs of the donor. Frequently donors will allow their names to be posted so that others who know them will be encouraged to join in the giving.

Whatever your personal opinion, it is important to mention that Jewish tradition does allow for public recognition of this kind. Ultimately, you yourself, will be the one to decide if this is to be a part of your own way of giving — in the form of plaques, lists of donors in newsletters, websites, or similar forms of publicity, or some other non-anonymous venue.

Should You Accept Tzedakah Money If You Need It?

Jewish tradition has a very clear position concerning making a living and the dignity of working to provide for one's own personal needs. To sustain oneself, a person should be willing to live sparingly if necessary, and should be prepared to do even menial work to be self-supporting. Three Talmudic texts teach:

ר׳ יהודה אמר: גדולה מלאכה שמכבדת את בעליה

Rabbi Yehuda said:
Work is noble — it gives dignity to the one who does it.

(Talmud Nedarim 49b)

רבי עקיבא היא דאמר: עשה שבתך חול ואל תצטרך לבריות

Rabbi Akiva said [referring to Shabbat meals]:
[If you have to], make your Shabbat [meal] like [those on] a week-day rather than ask for assistance from others.

(Talmud Shabbat 118a)

כדאמר ליה רב לרב כהנא:
נטוש נבילתא בשוקא ושקול אגרא
ולא תימא גברא רבא אנא וזילא בי מילתא

Rav said to Rav Kahana:
[If you have to,] take a job slaying animal carcasses in the marketplace, take your salary, but do not say, "I am a great man, and this is beneath my dignity."

(Talmud Bava Batra 110a)

Indeed, many of the Talmudic Rabbis had humble occupations, including woodcutters and shepherds. However, there are countless possible life situations when you might be unable to provide for yourself — either temporarily or permanently. What then? Based on Talmudic teachings, Maimonides unequivocally states Jewish tradition's position concerning taking Tzedakah when needed:

וכל מי שצריך ליטול ואינו יכול לחיות אלא אם כן נוטל
כגון זקן או חולה או בעל יסורין
ומגיס דעתו ואינו נוטל
הרי זה שופך דמים ומתחייב בנפשו
ואין לו בצערו אלא חטאות ואשמות

...and whoever needs to take Tzedakah, being unable to live without it — such as an elderly person or one who is sick or is suffering greatly — and who is too proud to take it — that person sheds blood and is to be held accountable, and there is no benefit from the suffering...only sin and guilt.

(Maimonides, Mishneh Torah,
Hilchot Matnot Ani'im, Laws of Gifts to Poor People, 10:19)

This is in sharp contrast to the often-quoted, "I would rather die than take charity." Judaism opposes this for two reasons: (1) What comparative benefit would there be to have a dead human being as opposed to one who is alive and capable of doing good for others, and (2) "Charity" in this statement implies a "hand-out". "Tzedakah", as you know, means "doing the right thing", a much different concept. "Tzedakah" also means "entitlement"; the recipient is entitled to receive the Tzedakah money. "Tzedakah" carries no implication whatsoever of degrading the recipient. The recipient and giver are equals: two human beings, both entitled to a decent, dignified life. You are not "doing a favor" for the person in need. You are both mutually part of the system that makes for Tikun Olam. My friend, Brayton Campbell, stated it beautifully, "Asking for help is a compliment to the person you are asking; it is not a sign of weakness." If you are truly in need, you should not feel that, in some way, you are doing something wrong by accepting Tzedakah money or that this is in any way contrary to Jewish law. Quite the opposite: Accepting Tzedakah when you need it is exactly what Jewish law prescribes.

Jewish tradition provides a classic real-life example of being a recipient:

אבל אסור לאכול משלו בסעודה ראשונה
Mourners are not allowed to eat their own food at the first meal [after the funeral].
(Shulchan Aruch, Yoreh De'ah 378:1)

Several profound insights are contained in this brief statement. Among them are:

1. The mourner has returned home from a second traumatic loss — first the death of the loved one, and then the terribly stark scene of the burial itself. And more, he or she has to turn away from the grave, leave the loved one behind, and then return to familiar surroundings, now empty of the deceased's presence.

2. The mourner is emotionally weakened and lonely. Returning home, he or she finds that everything has been prepared — the low bench or stool to sit on, and the food. Everything has been made ready by friends and members of the mourner's community, using their own money to provide the meal.

3. This meal has a special name that, in itself, reveals the nature of the Mitzvah. It is called סעודת ההבראה—Se'udat HaHavra'ah, the Havra'ah meal. הבראה—Havra'ah, means "recovery, healing, restoration-to-health". True, the food is intended to provide physical nutrition. Of greater

importance, though, is the fact that others are there for the mourner, to give the mourner strength by demonstrating that loneliness is not the human condition. People care, and they insist that the mourner know it, particularly at this most emotionally debilitating time in his or her personal life.

4. Perhaps most profound of all is Jewish tradition's assumption that the mourner is by nature a giving person. The lesson is: This is not the time to be a giver. The mourner must accept the community's acts of caring. Furthermore, knowing that the mourner is a giving person, tradition automatically frees him or her of the burden of having to ask others to help. It just happens. No questions asked.

Two analogies will further explain Judaism's position about accepting Tzedakah. The first is obvious: An ambulance speeding through red lights and traveling well beyond the posted speed limit is not breaking the law. It is doing what the law says it has to do to save a life. The second relates to people who have to eat on Yom Kippur, which is what Jewish tradition demands. This is corroborated by a story I heard about the great Torah genius, Rabbi Chaim Soloveitchik of Brisk. He was once asked why he was so lenient about permitting sick people to eat on Yom Kippur. He replied, "I am not lenient. On the contrary, I am quite strict when it comes to the Mitzvah of saving lives." Rabbi Soloveitchik's teaching is clear: If you need to take, you must take…and it most certainly does not violate the norms of Judaism. To the contrary, not taking would be contrary to Jewish principles.

If you still have hesitations about accepting Tzedakah, you should be aware that there is an additional option — interest-free loans. Interest-free loans have existed in Jewish life since Biblical times (see Leviticus 25:35-38). Jewish free-loan societies are located in many communities around North America, some of them more than 100 years old. www.freeloan.org is the website of the IAHFL, The International Association of Hebrew Free Loans, and it can provide you with useful information if you want to explore this option. Each society has its own procedures for providing loans, but every aspect of the society's work relating to the person seeking the loan is done with absolute confidentiality. Depending on its resources, each one, also, offers a wider or narrower type of loan, such as for emergency needs, business loans, or support for education and job training.

If you do decide to explore this option, be aware of three important incontrovertible facts: (1) The individuals who operate free-loan societies are an amazing group of sensitive, caring people; (2) the statistics show that more than 95% (and often 99% or more) of the loans are paid back. This demonstrates that they are operating extremely effectively, and (3) some of the free loan societies are large operations, others very small — but no matter what size they are, they share a common operational rule: Everyone who comes to them is treated with the utmost dignity.

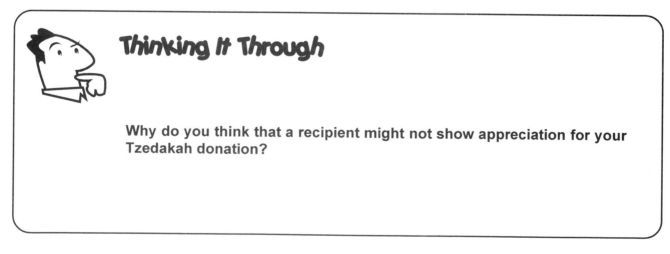

Thinking It Through

Why do you think that a recipient might not show appreciation for your Tzedakah donation?

Is It Possible to Do a "Pure" Act of Tzedakah With Your Money?

Yes.

Absolutely.

Having said that, the essential Tzedakah question is, "How do you determine if what you did with your Tzedakah money was a pure act of Tzedakah?"

I believe there are two criteria for determining the purity of the act: motive and expectation of return. Your possible motive for doing Tzedakah — because it is a Mitzvah, because you feel good, because it helps others, out of guilt or pity, etc. — is discussed in other parts of this guide. As for expectation of return, the Jewish answer is relatively simple: You should expect no thank-you from the recipient(s) and no public recognition for what you have done.

One Jewish text relates a curious and somewhat extreme tale of Tzedakah. (Jerusalem Talmud, Pe'ah, Chapter 8, end of Halachah 7) To paraphrase the story: One day, Rabbi Elazar came home and asked the members of his family what kind of Tzedakah they had done while he was gone. They answered that a group of hungry people had come by, and they had fed them. In gratitude, the wayfarers had prayed for Rabbi Elazar's continued wellbeing. The Rabbi was not at all pleased and told the family members that there was no good reward for their act. Another time he came home and asked the same question. They gave the same answer, but this time the guests had cursed the Rabbi. The Rabbi told the members of his family that that kind of response indicated that their Mitzvah-act had been pure.

Again, this is certainly an extreme example. Nevertheless, in the same section of the Talmud, the following is told:

ר"ע בעין ממניתיה פרנס
א"ל נמלך גו ביתא
הלכון בתריה שמעון קליה דימור
על מנת מקל על מנת מבזייא

Members of his community wanted to appoint
Rabbi Akiva manager of the community's Tzedakah fund.
He said to them, "I want to go home and consult with the members of my family."
They followed him [to his home] and overheard,
"[Know that you] will be humiliated and maligned."

(Jerusalem Talmud, Pe'ah, Chapter 8, end of Halachah 7)

The language of the ancient text is problematical. "פרנס–Parnass" can mean either "community leader" or "manager of the community's Tzedakah funds." It is also possible that the closing line means that Rabbi Akiva said to his family, "I am accepting this position fully aware that I may be humiliated and maligned", and thereby telling them not to be concerned about the criticisms that will possibly come with the position.

Still, it would seem natural that the recipient ought to show some appreciation for what you have done. You should keep in mind, though, that there are several legitimate reasons why some kind of "thank-you" might not be forthcoming. While your initial reaction may be that the recipient is ungrateful, that is certainly not always true.

Why Might a Recipient be Silent?

Some of the following circumstances may explain the reason for the silence:

1. The recipients may be too embarrassed to respond. This is a common and very real aspect of the relationship of recipients to donors. It happens all the time.

2. To preserve their own dignity, the recipients just cannot communicate with the giver in any way.

3. By their very nature, the recipients may just be inarticulate people or, unable to express themselves.

4. The recipients, even though generally articulate, may be experiencing "first-time recipient syndrome". They have never had to take from others before, and, in addition, they may have never had to ask for anything from others before.

5. There may have been some glitch in communication. You know this from everyday life — for whatever reason, a letter just never got to you, or an e-mail got lost in cyberspace or disappeared when your computer crashed. It is possible that some Mitzvah-intermediary — perhaps the person who delivered the furniture you anonymously bought for a family in need — forgot to tell you that the single mother expressed appreciation what you had done for her family.

6. Furthermore, the recipients may have profound psychological scars which you could not possibly comprehend, even if you were the most skilled therapist. (In this situation you most certainly can understand why the recipients do not express their gratitude.)

All of these are valid possibilities, but whatever the reason or reasons, "thank you" is not your issue. It is enough for you to know that you recognized another person's need, responded to it, and did the right thing by using your money for an act of Tzedakah.

Postscript: A New Term

In the realm of Gemillut Chassadim, i.e., using your non-monetary effort, time, or talents for others, there is a particularly rich Jewish term, חסד של אמת – Chessed shel Emet, a true act of caring lovingkindness. The Talmud explains that burying someone is a Chessed shel Emet because there is absolutely no possibility of a return, reward, or thank-you from that person. What is described above about Tzedakah money would then be צדקה של אמת –Tzedakah shel Emet, true, pure Tzedakah.

How Did/ Do You Feel When?

Reviewing your previous experiences doing Mitzvahs and giving Tzedakah, how do you compare the frequency and intensity of strong emotions in your "regular life" to those when you are engaged in Tikun Olam?

Using the chart below, evaluate each listed emotional response, and using a scale of 1-5 (with 5 being the most frequent or intense and 1 being the least) rate your experiences. Feel free to make additional notes as you explore your memories.

Emotional Response	Rating in Your Regular Life (1-5)	Rating While Doing Tikun Olam (1-5)	Notes (what was happening that made you feel this way?)
I hug			
I laugh			
I cry			
I weep over			
I feel good			
I get excited			
I lose sleep			
I feel tired			
I worry			
I feel needed			
I feel "down"			
I feel exhilarated			

Reviewing the results of your comparisons above, what have you learned or remembered about yourself?

How can your review of these comparisons lead you to give more Tzedakah?

Why is there no Bracha before doing an act of Tzedakah?

Sometimes it seems that there is a special blessing for everything in Judaism: before eating a sandwich, when celebrating a momentous event in life, on week-days, Shabbat, and holidays, seeing a rainbow, landing in Israel... The list goes on and on. It is true that there are several Mitzvah acts and occasions for which there is no prescribed blessing. Nevertheless, many people I talk to find it particularly curious why there is no Bracha before doing an act of Tzedakah. You would think that, for such an important Jewish and human action, it should be honored or sanctified by a blessing of praise or thanks. Over the past several years, I have asked dozens of people why they think this is so. Usually, I get the best answers when I ask the question "out of the blue". This allows them to give their first spontaneous answer.

Blessings For Everything

Look at Birkot HaShachar- the morning blessings in the beginning of the siddur that we recite each day. There is a blessing for everything!

Why do you think there is no Bracha when we give Tzedakah?

If you were to design a Bracha, what would it be? If a Bracha does not work, what might you include in a prayer?

In no particular order, some of the answers I have received include:

1. If you are concentrating on making the blessing, you may be interfering with giving your Tzedakah properly and efficiently. Or you may be so focused on doing the act of Tzedakah just right, you may make a mistake when you recite the blessing. Both of these are particularly true for people who often have to grope and fumble to remember the right words or who are not skilled "multi-taskers".

2. Probably the most powerful one I have heard: There are times when there is not a second to lose. Many Tzedakah situations require an immediate response. Delay of any kind may have serious consequences, including embarrassment to the person in need or even loss of life because of that split-second delay. The need to be prepared at all times is illustrated by a Talmudic story about the sage Rabbi Chana bar Chanila'i

ולא שקל ידא מן כיסא דסבר דילמא אתי עני בר טובים
ואדמטו לי לכיסא קא מכסיף

who always kept a hand in his pocket, thinking, "A poor person who was once financially stable may come along, and by the time I reach into my pocket to give, the person may feel humiliated."

(Berachot 58b)

3. A psychological approach: Since it often seems that giving money away goes against the grain of human nature, there is no need to recite a blessing. You are taking this most common and frequently-misused thing — money — and using it for a holy purpose. How could you not know that this act is something special? Therefore, my interpreter-friend explained, there is no need for a Bracha to remind you that you are engaged in something sacred.

4. There is the slightest chance that personal pride may intrude when you are engaged in an act of Tzedakah. You might think, "I [i.e., Big Me, Look at me!] am going to do something so important that there is even a Bracha assigned to it". That would shift the focus too much to the donor, rather than to the recipient.

5. My friend and teacher, Rabbi Neal Gold, made reference to a Torah-insight by the Chassidic Rebbi Simcha Bunem. The Rebbi taught that one who needs to make a Bracha may not consider himself or herself "clean" enough to pronounce such holy words. Therefore, there is no Bracha, and the person should respond immediately to the need. Rabbi Gold offers three contemporary interpretations of "not 'clean' enough": 1) lacking the self-confidence to make a difference, (2) lacking the perspective that one is capable of making a difference, and (3) thinking to one's self, "There are others who do this so much better than I do." Therefore, Rabbi Bunem is saying, "Remove all hesitation, doubt, and comparisons, and do something."

6. My friend and teacher, Louise Cohen, sent me a particularly eloquent and profound possible answer:

In general, Brachas make us more conscious of God's gifts to us, so we pause to sanctify moments in time, food, etc. But maybe it's better not to be so "conscious" of the fact that we are giving Tzedakah. Champion figure skaters and other athletes talk about "skating dumb" and "muscle memory". By the time they are in competition, they stop "thinking", intellectualizing, and analyzing what they need to do to perform their amazing leaps and spins. It becomes not just what they do but also who they are. Similarly, giving Tzedakah should become part of what we do and who we are. Instead of wasting time verbalizing the holiness of the act, we should just do it. We say blessings at the beginning of each day, thanking God for making us who we are, then we go about our day. Ideally, we could say a blessing before the gift of each brand new breath we inhale and exhale, but that wouldn't be a sane way to live. Just as we are creatures that live by breathing in and out — and our other blessings acknowledge that we don't take this for granted — we should also be creatures for whom giving Tzedakah is an organic, almost biological component of who we are, and it is covered under our general daily blessings.

These six interpretations barely scratch the surface. Perhaps it would be beneficial now and again to ask ourselves the same question, "Why is there no blessing before doing an act of Tzedakah?" Each new answer yields new meanings, and each one enriches the experience and adds to the power of the act itself.

PART THREE
Exactly How Do You Decide Where to Donate Your Money?

Evaluating Tzedakot

Is it enough that "they" are doing good things— Why should trustworthiness be your ultimate concern when you donate your money to Tzedakah?

The short answer is, "No."

When I review the many letters and e-mails I get from rabbis, educators, and friends that report where they have sent their Tzedakah money, two questions come to my mind:

1. Is it enough that the organizations that receive their Tzedakah money are doing good things, or is there something more that we should expect from them?

2. Have the rabbis, educators, and friends done their homework? By this I mean — did they check the organizations out sufficiently, i.e., do they really know *exactly* what these recipient-groups will be doing with the Tzedakah money they are soliciting? The short answer to this one is "often they do not."

Both of these are crucial issues, and will be discussed in subsequent chapters.

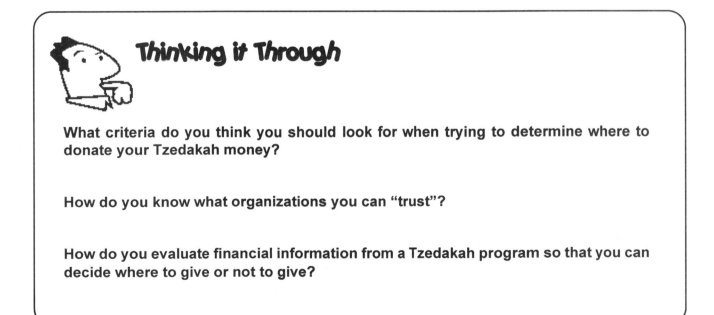

Thinking it Through

What criteria do you think you should look for when trying to determine where to donate your Tzedakah money?

How do you know what organizations you can "trust"?

How do you evaluate financial information from a Tzedakah program so that you can decide where to give or not to give?

Simulation Allocations Project

Allocating Tzedakah funds is not an easy process. There are so many organizations and people in the world who are in need. How can you ever decide that one is more important than the next?

If you had collected some Tzedakah funds and wanted to contribute them, how would you decide who deserves your support?

Let's say that you decided to contribute to Jewish needs. Since you have a limited amount of funds, you need to prioritize.

Consider the list below. Treat it like a score-card or a ratings sheet. You have a total of 20 points to distribute and cannot distribute more than 5 points to any of the categories on the list. How would you rate the following:

_____	Israel
_____	The Conservative Movement
_____	Jewish Child Care, Children, Elderly, Counseling
_____	Jewish medical needs
_____	Jewish people with disabilities, blind
_____	World Jewish community

Many synagogues and Jewish communities have their own Tzedakah funds. (For example, USY has its Tikun Olam Tzedakah Fund). Usually these groups need to decide how to allocate the Tzedakah funds they have collected.

We have chosen fifteen Tzedakot (organizations, institutions, or programs which receive Tzedakah funds) from a list of over sixty which have received support from USY's Tikun Olam Tzedakah Fund. Let's assume that you have collected $20,000 for distribution. After considering each organization and the funding they have requested for specific projects, how will you divide the money you have available? Remember, you have a total of $20,000.

ORGANIZATIONS TO CONSIDER AND GRANT REQUESTS

1. **ABAYUDAYA JEWISH COMMUNITY IN UGANDA** —This Jewish community in Uganda has been practicing Judaism as they always have, devoutly, spiritually, and disconnected from the world wide Jewish community. The Tikun Olam money raised for Abayudaya community goes directly to these Jews, primarily for books and education.
   REQUESTED GRANT: $3,000 to purchase more books for library; $10,000 to build Yeshiva building which will house the library.

2. **ALYN**—The Alyn Woldenberg Orthopedic Hospital and Rehabilitation Center for physically handicapped children in Israel treats patients up to 18 years of age, offering physiotherapy, occupational therapy and treatment to disabled children. Alyn services 100 in-patients, 20 day patients and has a lengthy waiting list
   REQUESTED GRANT: $1,500 for hospital bed; $1,500 for materials for active rehabilitation ward

3. **AUSCHWITZ JEWISH CENTER FOUNDATION**—Founded in 1992 when New York business-men found that there was no appropriate place for people to mourn and reflect when visiting the Auschwitz Concentration Camp, the Foundation's mission is to ensure that there will be a lasting Jewish presence in the nearby city of Oswiecim (Auschwitz). The Foundation's activities are centered around the preservation of the only remaining synagogue building in Auschwitz, Chevra Lomdei Mishnayot, and the building of an educational and resource center in an adjacent former Jewish family home. The exhibits in the Center concentrate on the story of Jewish life in the area prior to the Holocaust.

    REQUESTED GRANT: $6,000 to underwrite one Auschwitz Fellow; $2,000 for Polish, German, and Hebrew subtitles for DVD; $1,500 for signs to make people aware of AJC at the camp

4. **CHAI LIFELINE/ "CAMP SIMCHA"**—Chai Lifeline is designed to help Jewish patients and families of those dealing with cancer and other life-threatening diseases. The camp then offers these children a chance to get away from home and feel/act like the children they are, with specific care for their health needs, while offering their families a respite from caring for them. All programs are offered free of charge.

    REQUESTED GRANT: $1,000 to help purchase new arcade games

5. **ISRAEL FREE LOAN ASSOCIATION**—This is an interest-free loan fund for people in Israel. Examples of purposes for which loans are given include emergency and unanticipated expenses, health and dental treatment, school supplies, food, clothing, basic furniture and utensils, basic household repairs, interest on debts such as mortgage payments, extra hours of homemaker service for the ill and homebound, expenses for Jewish holidays, college tuition, day care and other basic needs. Maximum grants are up to $1,000 per family.

    REQUESTED GRANT: Requested money for loans.

6. **ISRAEL GUIDE DOG CENTER FOR THE BLIND**—Founded in 1991 the Israel Guide Dog Center's mission is to help blind people in Israel achieve independence and mobility. Prior to the opening of the Center, blind Israelis had to travel to the United States to get guide dogs. Aside from being prohibitively expensive for most Israelis the situation also posed a language barrier challenge both for the clients as well as the dogs that had been trained in English. The Center breeds and trains dogs as well as provides follow-up care for all of its clients to make sure the partnership is working.

    REQUESTED GRANT: $1,000 for two puppy sponsorships

7. **ISRAEL NATIONAL THERAPEUTIC RIDING ASSOCIATION**—The former Therapeutic Riding Club was established in 1986. Its purpose is to promote the recovery of disabled individuals through horseback riding, support related medical research and to train and certify therapeutic riding instructors. Therapeutic riding helps improve muscle tone, balance, posture, coordination, motor development and emotional and physical well-being.

    REQUESTED GRANT: $2,500 for a saddle for psychotic and mentally ill clients

8. **JERUSALEM SHELTER FOR BATTERED WOMEN**—In operation since 1981, Beit Zipporah is a shelter in Jerusalem for battered women and their children. They have been able to provide shelter for over fifty families a year. No matter how long each woman stays in the shelter, the fact that she has been there and has begun to break through the wall of secrecy and silence and shame gives her strength to face her future choices, and to make choices independently.

    REQUESTED GRANT: $3,000 for Therapeutic Counseling project

9. **JEWISH BRAILLE INSTITUTE OF AMERICA**—Centered in New York, the Jewish Braille Institute provides services for the Jewish Blind throughout North America. This includes religious training through tapes and transcription of Braille materials in Hebrew such as Siddurim and Chumashim.

    REQUESTED GRANT: $1,800 to expand Braille library

10. **MAGEN DAVID ADOM**—As Israel's equivalent to the Red Cross, Magen David Adom has provided emergency medical aid wherever and whenever needed, through its 75 branches. It runs the only blood fractionation and processing plant in Israel, and provides concentrated training in first aid techniques and emergency treatment. When there is a terrorist attack in Israel, Magen David Adom is always first on the scene to save lives.

    REQUESTED GRANT: $5,000 for Sderot MDA Emergency Medical Station Building; $5,000 to purchase blood bag supplies for national center

11. **MASORTI OLAMI**—Masorti Olami strives to create Conservative (or "Masorti") Jewish communities wherever Jews live in order to combat the disappearance of young Jews seeking to "blend in" with their peers. They do this by setting up Masorti synagogues, schools, camps, NOAM youth groups and MAROM young leadership networks everywhere Jews reside: Western and Central Europe, Eastern Europe and the FSU, Latin America, Australia and South Africa.

    REQUESTED GRANT: $3,500 for Youth leadership development in Nice, France; $3,000 for Ulpan in Moscow, Russia; $3,000 for Counselor Training in Buenos Aries, Argentina

12. **NATIONAL TAY SACHS FOUNDATION**—This non-profit, philanthropic organization was formed to raise funds for, and to promote research into Tay-Sachs and allied neurodegenerative diseases of infancy and childhood; to support and promote programs of carrier detection and prevention; and to assist the families of afflicted children by making available to them counseling facilities, out-patient clinics and the opportunity to participate in the purposes and programs of the association.

    REQUESTED GRANT: $3,000 to underwrite a portion of family conference

13. **PROJECT EZRA**—Designed to work with Jewish aged and poor on New York's Lower East Side and based in a local synagogue, the program consists of providing companionship as well as physical assistance on a one-to one basis. Many of the people helped by Project Ezra are elderly Russian Jews who receive little or no assistance from the US government. Project Ezra provides them with free transportation, Russian-speaking facilitators and social workers, and free meals to those who wouldn't otherwise be able to afford Shabbat meals.

    REQUESTED GRANT: $3000 to fund van trips with lunch. $500 for 5 Shabbat meals.

14. **RABANIT BRACHA KAPACH**—The Rabanit (Rabbi's Wife) takes care of hundreds of people throughout the Nachalat Shiva neighborhood of Jerusalem, as well as other neighborhoods. She provides wedding dresses for brides who cannot afford their own, summer camping for kids and Shabbat provisions for poor families.

    REQUESTED GRANT: $2500 to fund Passover meal project.

15. **YAD SARAH**—A voluntary organization in Israel, with centers throughout the country, Yad Sarah provides medical equipment on loan to all who require it, asking only a nominal fully refundable deposit. Yad Sarah centers are open round the clock to provide for emergencies.

    REQUESTED GRANT: $1600 to purchase blood pressure cuffs.

ALLOCATIONS WORKSHEET

ORGANIZATION	AMOUNT ALLOCATED ($)	PURPOSE OF FUNDS
1. ABAYUDAYA JEWISH COMMUNITY IN UGANDA		
2. ALYN		
3. AUSCHWITZ JEWISH CENTER FOUNDATION		
4. CHAI LIFELINE/ "CAMP SIMCHA"		
5. ISRAEL FREE LOAN ASSOCIATION		
6. ISRAEL GUIDE DOG CENTER FOR THE BLIND		
7. ISRAEL NATIONAL THERAPEUTIC RIDING ASSOCIATION		
8. JERUSALEM SHELTER FOR BATTERED WOMEN		
9. JEWISH BRAILLE INSTITUTE OF AMERICA		
10. MAGEN DAVID ADOM		
11. MASORTI OLAMI		
12. NATIONAL TAY SACHS FOUNDATION		
13. PROJECT EZRA		
14. RABANIT BRACHA KAPACH		
15. YAD SARAH		

TOTAL AMOUNT ALLOCATED: $

 Now that you have made the first attempt to allocate funds, what points did you consider when reaching your decisions?

Consider the following questions:
1. Is it better to give to local Tzedakot than ones that are far away?
2. How will your dollars impact the organization?
3. Will the organization be able to function without your dollars?

Now, review the list and your allocations, and see if you want to change anything.

Once you have made your final decisions, please consider the following:

1. Was it difficult to decide which organizations would receive your funds?
2. If there are any which didn't receive any of your Tzedakah money, why did you reach that decision?
3. How did it feel to make these decisions?
4. What information/ criteria did you want to know about each agency before determining funding?

What Is the Fundamental Jewish Text About Trust?

Common sense should tell you that you would want and need to know how your money is being used. This is true in both areas where money makes a difference, i.e., money for your own personal needs, and, no less, for Tzedakah.

Let us say some of the lights begin to flicker in your house. You call the electrician, settle on the cost, and this expert examines and repairs what needs to be fixed. When the process is over, you will want to know not only that everything works properly, but also that the house is safe from an electrical fire. That is what you paid for. Consequently, you can go to the beach or visit your favorite Uncle Sholom Dov for a week without fear that the house will be destroyed because of some mishap in your home's wiring system. That is what you paid for.

It makes sense.

Tzedakah works the same way. You want to change the world by making someone else's life, in some way, better than it is. You will then begin to search for a Mitzvah hero, an organization, or a cause that does just that — makes lives better. Because so much is at stake, you will most definitely want to make certain that the people you are dealing with are absolutely reliable.

It makes sense.

It is simple logic, common sense.

 My friend, Sharon Halper, gave this procedure a name — The Rule of the Three E's: Is any recipient of your Tzedakah going to use the money **E**fficiently and **E**ffectively, and will they use it **E**xactly as they said they would. Jewish tradition has considerable literature concerning the responsibility of the donor and the recipient. Maimonides' summarizes it in his Mishneh Torah Law Code (Laws of Gifts to Poor People, Chapter 10):

ולא יתן אדם לתוך קופה של צדקה
אלא אם כן יודע שהממונה נאמן וחכם ויודע להנהיג כשורה...

...one should not give to a Tzedakah fund unless the donor knows that the person responsible is ....trustworthy, wise [in managing and distributing the funds], and acts with the absolute integrity...

To understand the full implications of this text, it is best to break it down into two areas: (1) the managers, board of directors, and any others involved in collecting and distributing the funds and directing the program activities, and (2) the organization's overall finances.

Why Is the Hebrew Root "אמן-Amen" the Same As for "נאמן-Trustworthy" The Same?

אמן–Amen

You have heard the word since you were a child. And you hear it everywhere. You hear it in synagogue (where you would expect to hear it) and you hear it outside of the sanctuary walls. You are not surprised to hear a talk show host respond to a caller by saying, "Ay-men to that, buddy."

Being a student of words, I began to look into the meaning of this very short, very powerful word. It didn't take long before I discovered that its essential meaning is "firm, strong", and saying "Amen" meant that we confirm or affirm what someone else had just said, proclaimed, or offered in prayer. Digging a little deeper, I learned that אמן-Amen is related to ימן – the root of the word "ימין–right hand". Throughout the millennia-long history of the Hebrew language, this word became a synonym for "strength, power". Other languages also favored the right hand. In Latin, "dexter" eventually became "dextrous" in English. The French, "droite" became our "adroit", skillful. The opposite — "left" — developed negative connotations. In Latin it is "sinister", in French, "gauche". You need only ask Elders if any of them who were born left-handed were forced by their parents to write with their right hand.

"Right" is good; "left" is to be avoided at all costs.

This is exactly why "אמן" and its cousin "ימן" are so important in the world of Tzedakah. Maimonides' text quoted in a previous chapter gives three crucial criteria for those in charge of any Tzedakah program: They must be נאמנים– trustworthy, wise [in managing and distributing the funds], and must act with absolute integrity. You would want to add, also, that the supervisors are Menschen and treat the recipients and their employees decently and fairly.

Even without any reference to Jewish texts, it should be obvious why you would want to know about the character of the directors and the staff members who manage Tzedakah money. You have to trust them. This Mitzvah money is meant to better the lives of others. More than your plumber or car mechanic, they have to know what they are doing because the stakes are so high. They have the power of life and death no less than the heart surgeon who replaces a valve. And, not least of all, they ought to be the kind of person you like and respect as a human being.

Will Your Tzedakah Money Have a Greater Impact If You Give Larger Amounts to a Single Tikun Olam Program Rather Than Smaller Amounts to Many?

Sometimes yes and sometimes no.

For Small Sums — Part I – the "No":

Your pattern of giving may include giving at least some small amoun Tzedakah every time you are asked. This may include personal solicita tions, phone calls, e-mails, or snail-mail requests. The importance of do ing research about these solicitations is covered in other chapters in this book. Those selections will cover how to prevent an unreasonably large percentage of your Tzedakah dollar from being wasted. This chapter is concerned with donating small sums to Mitzvah heroes and organiza tions you have already researched.

For Small Sums — Part II — the "Yes":

When you have discovered Mitzvah heroes and programs that change the lives of others for the better with $5.00, $2.00, $1.00, even 50¢ — then making many small donations is entirely appropriate. And more — not only is it entirely appropriate, it should become a regular facet of your personal Tzedakah program.

The section— What Possible Difference Could $38.00, $22.00, $18.00–Even $2.66–Make in Someone's Life? — discusses in detail how small sums of Tzedakah money can and do make miracles happen. Keep in mind that becoming accustomed to this aspect of Tzedakah also serves as a constant re minder of the awesome power of Mitzvah money to do incredible quantities of good.

For Large Sums:

Suppose you want to buy school supplies or provide hot lunches for a group of students whose fami lies do not have enough money. And, let us say you have done your research and are satisfied that the organization is doing the program economically and efficiently. If the group says that the program will not happen at all unless X dollars are collected, then it makes sense to contribute all, or a large percentage of, your Tzedakah budget to this one worthy program. If, however, you have done your research and "something doesn't feel right" about what you have discovered, even if you have enor mous sums to give away, then, even though the absolute value of your Tzedakah money may be very high — $25,000, $100,000, $1,000,000 — the true Tikun Olam value may fall to near-zero or absolute nil.

You could allow Libby Reichman's Big Brothers Big Sisters of Israel to triple the number of at-risk children it reaches. For decades into the future, many lives could be changed. "Many lives" means not only the lives of the "Little Brothers" and "Little Sisters", but also the lives of thousands of others they will encounter over those future years of living a better life. Their lives, too, will be better because of your well-timed and well-placed Tzedakah. (http://www.bigbrothers.org.il/)

And, as for example: You could make the dreams come true for hundreds or thousands of Elders in closed-care institutions by donating and working with PK Beville and Second Wind Dreams. (www.secondwind.org)

And, as for example: If you (1) are very thorough in your research, (2) find a Mitzvah hero whose Tikun Olam work appeals to you spiritually, existentially, and intellectually, and (3) you don't necessarily need to worry about tax deductions, then you can call that Mitzvah hero and say, "What can $50,000 do for you?" Give and take and refine the match of needs to funds, then just do it.

And, as for example…

And, as for example…

By then, you will be "on a roll" and one glorious Mitzvah will lead to another and to another and to yet another.

In Sum: How Much Is a "Large Sum"? a "Small Sum"? and What About "Medium Sums?"

Your personal understanding of "small sums" and "large sums" will depend on your own Tzedakah budget. (And depending on that absolute figure, you will also be able to determine how much is available in the category of "medium sums".)

Most likely, you will want to do all kinds of Tzedakah — small and medium, and large, if "large" is within your range. All amounts of Tzedakah money will and do change lives, and all — when done right — are equally valid. Every Tzedakah dollar has the power to change lives for the better, and, indeed, to make miracles happen.

How Should You Do Tzedakah If You Happen to Have More Money Than God, or As Much, or Almost As Much Money as God?

You could...

You could wipe out a disease that ravages millions of people's lives. Bill and Melinda Gates and Bono have taken the initiative in this vast area of Tikun Olam.

You could join them in this effort.

> You can make sure that every kid in your community gets a free Jewish day school education.

> > You can.

> > > You might fund 50,000 people to be tested as potential bone marrow donors. Each one just might save a life.

You could establish institutes in Israel and North America to train people in doing Earthshaking Tzedakah. The program would focus on students meeting Mitzvah heroes, learning from these Distinguished Teachers of Tikun Olam, and then joining them in their work. Your budget could cover not only constructing and maintaining the buildings, but also setting up an endowment. The staff could then do its holy work without ever needing to worry about raising funds for operations. The total package probably wouldn't take more than $5,000,000 or $10,000,000.

You could do it.

You could do it if that's what appeals to you.

It might even be "a piece of cake" for you.

You could travel to Israel and ask every one of the Mitzvah heroes what they need to make every one of their dreams come true. And not just their temporary or mid-range measures to gain stability just for now. For the ones who are inspired and inspiring but can't seem to do anything administrative, you can buy them assistants and infrastructure so that they can be totally left to do what they do best, namely, change lives according to their vision and talents. For example, you could build a facility for Anita Shkedi and her Israel National Therapeutic Riding Association (INTRA), and provide for all her other needs: additional staff to manage the operation, and provide enough money where she could advertise, "Let all those in need of body-and-soul repair come to us." (www.intra.org.il)

You could, if that appeals to you. It certainly is a critical need.

And you could do it without any desire to exert personal control, because you know the Mitzvah heroes will make wise use of your money.

You could just walk into the home of a Mitzvah hero whose Tikun Olam work you have researched carefully, hand over a check for $1,000,000 — no questions asked — then ride off into the sunset on your white horse with a mighty "Hi ho, Silver, away!"

You could establish a new Mitzvah program to replace one that is too inefficient or wasteful.

You could, and you would feel very good about it, because you were making it happen more efficiently, more economically, and more people would have better lives because of it.

You could pick up the phone and call a friend who also has more than, as much as, or nearly as much money as God and say, "Sophie, please sit down with Miriam and tell her that I am putting in $4,000,000 for Jewish Elders in the Former Soviet Union. Massive numbers of them are living on $30- and $40-a-month pensions. I want to give them the kind of money that will let them get their medicines, better food, a chance to go outside for a stroll in the Springtime…and a chance to be happy. Discuss it, but don't discuss it to death. I already have the perfect Mitzvah hero who can reach hundreds of people, so there won't be any worry about anything going to waste. See if she likes the idea and if the two of you would like to match my $4,000,000." (Visit www.amechad.org and learn of Igor Feldblyum's fine work in this area of Tikun Olam.)

You could do it. Millionaires and billionaires do it all the time, and you could feel "double extra" good because you have doubled your Mitzvah money by making just one phone call.

Whatever it is, do it because (1) it is something that you personally like, (2) it is desperately needed, or, best of all, (3) you have reached a point in your Tzedakah giving to realize it has to be some combination of (1) and (2). With that much money you have already come to realize that it isn't enough just to base your miracle-work on personal preference. There has to be something more.

You Could Do it With the Help of People who "get it", i.e.,

… people who know how Tzedakah money works miracles and changes the lives of people in need

… people who have the human touch

… people who are constantly aware that, while your endeavors are potentially dripping with all the pitfalls of a "power trip", they have a firm grip on the truth: Tikun Olam is humbling and, Fixing the World is all about humility

… people who "get" who you are, always respect your own Self, and never overstep their bounds when helping you to put your Tzedakah money to work best. You certainly could do Tzedakah better with these fine people at your side.

You Could Do It Without the Help of

… some social investment entrepreneurs who have brought the good message of sound business management to Mitzvah work, but who may have gone too far in their theoretical transfer of principles. They may have forgotten that Mitzvah work and business principles don't always overlap. They may not be focusing enough on human needs. There may be occasions when "risk" means something different. They may not have had enough experience in Tikun Olam to understand that "cost effectiveness" is often, but not *always*, a primary consideration. It is possible that, when it comes to Mitzvahs, they haven't yet grasped the proper balance between rational long-term planning and "gut feeling". Many times they do it out of innocence, but, whatever the reason, you will probably do better without their help if they seem too absolutist about their theories.

… a few — probably more than a few — people who make their living by slick presentations to people just like yourselves. They are the ones you read about who scan the newspapers for lottery winners. Some are expert hucksters, and others are classic shysters and frauds. No doubt you can do a lot better without them if they suddenly appear at your door.

No doubt, you have already given away serious money to Tzedakah. Along the way you may have been burned once or twice. Be aware that there are many people who can work with you that do not fall into any of the previous categories.

A Story: Paul Newman

Think about Paul Newman, actor, director, race car driver…and Big Time Tzedakah Man. By 2006, he had given away more than $200,000,000. Everyone knows the story:

"Gee, Paul, you ought to sell this yummy salad dressing of yours."
"I'll do it, but let's take all of the money I make and give it away to Tzedakah."

Read the labels on his products. There's a nice touch of humor to each one. You see it at www.newmansown.com and other resources. "Paul Newman, as sole owner of Newman's Own™, donates all his after-tax profits to educational and charitable purposes." Nice, but even nicer is the line, "Newman's Own: Shameless Exploitation In Pursuit of The Common Good." It's the same style of humor that we remember from Butch Cassidy and The Sundance Kid. Paul contributes to hundreds of Tzedakah projects. I haven't checked lately, but, a few years ago, I read an article that reported he is directly involved in the giving, and that the Newman's Own Tzedakah staff has a good sense of how to do it. But even allowing for a 2% or 3% "unwise staff hiring" record, he has done much better than others who don't have quite as much money as God, but still enough to do a multitude of divine Mitzvahs.

A Second Story: Eugene Lang
More than 20 years ago, Eugene Lang was asked to give a speech to a 6th grade graduating class. The school was in East Harlem where he, himself, had been a student years before. In the interim, the neighborhood had changed and the student population was composed mostly of disadvantaged and at-risk kids. Shortly before Mr. Lang delivered his talk, he had a revelation. He set aside his prepared speech, and, instead, spoke from the heart. He promised that he would send any students to college who would graduate from high school.

The "I Have a Dream Foundation" was born, and its website, which reviewed the background for the 1995 Presidential Medal of Freedom that he received states, "IHAD currently supports 150 projects in 57 cities nationwide. More than 200 sponsors have helped more than 12,000 disadvantaged students with academic support and guidance from elementary school through their high school years."

I still haven't met Mr. Lang. Nor have I met Paul Newman (though I drove by his house once). They're both on my "Some Day" calendar. Soon, I hope.

Extreme Wealth
You know the stories about various idiosyncrasies and often severely-misplaced values of some super-wealthy people. Recently, I heard one from a friend. He told me about a woman who had millions in the bank, and a money market fund with more than $500,000. She used this account for writing personal checks. My friend told me that this woman would fly into an absolute panic when the account dipped below $500,000. She was terrified that she was running out of ready cash.

There are tales in every body of literature about rich people who are very stingy when it comes to Tzedakah. One of my favorite Chassidic stories is about a Rebbi who summons a rich man to his house to teach a lesson about giving. First he takes him to a window and asks, "What do you see?" The rich man replies, "I see some people taking a leisurely stroll. Others are going into shops and buying things. To the right are some kids playing in the square." The Rebbi then takes him to a mirror and asks, "What do you see?" The rich man answers, "I see myself." The Rebbi then says, "See — the window is made of glass, but add a little silver to it, and you stop seeing other people. You see only yourself."

As I said, when I was writing this chapter, I wasn't even thinking of the classic "stingy rich person" theme. There are just too many people out there with oodles, tons, and semi-truckloads of money who are making Mitzvahs happen Big Time.

One Final Thought
You may be one of the few who has millions, tens of millions, hundreds of millions, or a billion or two at your disposal. I have had some contact with individuals such as yourselves, and I would only add this: While you are thinking about and doing Very Big Mitzvahs, keep in mind that you can also make some "small" or medium-size Tikun Olam happen. There is a certain fascination about giving away a million here and a million there, but also remember to be on the lookout for opportunities where $10,000, $25,000 or $50,000 will make the difference. For you, it may be no more difficult than just writing a check. But for the Mitzvah hero and his or her work, for other Tikun Olam programs, or for other recipients, it will save hours, weeks, perhaps months of work, anguish, and unnecessary suffering. This is just one more aspect of your Mitzvah work that can give you a unique sense of satisfaction.

There are, of course, in addition a hefty number of situations where $100, $180, $250, or $500 could change someone's life completely.

Indeed, your Tzedakah work could be very rich, combining Colossal-Sized Tzedakah, Medium-Range Tzedakah, and Small Tzedakah (which never is "small". Never.)

You could do it. No doubt about it.

The only thing left to do is to do it.

One More Final Thought
eMarketer is a website devoted to "daily coverage of the latest e-business data and eMarketer analysis." A May 19, 2005, report stated that Baby Boomers have $1,000,000,000,000 (that's $1 trillion) in buying power. Other sources estimate an even more staggering figure. As best as I can tell, whatever the precise number might be, it sounds like "almost as much money as God has" in the celestial bank at any one time. The writer is, of course, referring to the classical definition of "Baby Boomer", i.e., North Americans born between 1946 and 1964. He doesn't break it down by age sub-groups, but I would suspect that even a small percentage of $1 trillion held by the older Boomers can do an incredible amount of Tikun Olam.

What Possible Difference Could $38, $22, $18 — Even $2.66 — Make in Someone Else's Life?

וצדקה תציל ממות
Tzedakah saves from death.
(Proverbs 10:2)

If You Have Already Read the Chapter about People Who Have More Money Than God — Then
You may be feeling frustrated or inadequate. You may be thinking that the only way to change the world is with millions, billions, or gazillions of dollars. Don't despair and don't even think twice about it. There are not only as many ways to do Tikun Olam with small sums of money as there are by huge sums, in reality, there are many more of them. I dropped out of college math after two semesters of calculus, so I am not certain if there are infinitely more. But there are many, many, many more.

Report from Arnie Draiman
Arnie Draiman is Ziv Tzedakah Fund's representative in Israel. We exchange e-mails many times a day, with phone calls scattered over time depending on the need. Among other things, he loves to play a role in small–money high–impact Mitzvahs. When I told him I was considering doing a short piece about $5.00, $10.00, $25.00 Mitzvahs, he sent me the following report. It is unedited, except for certain details that he and I changed to preserve the confidentiality and anonymity of the recipients:

Real live ones in the last several months:

under $100 —
$72 –winter electric bill for elderly person ([we do] many elec bills for many people)
$61–phone bill for survivor of terror ([we do] many phone bills)
$96–pair of comfortable sneakers for survivor of terror (with foot pain)
$85–taking a small family of a survivor out to dinner - woman so enthralled by actually going out again she stayed up the night before sewing/making a new dress for the "occasion"
$78–good chair for a desk for a college student survivor of terror
$55–school uniforms for children from survivor of terror family
$85–for new holiday clothes
$80–grocery scrip (can come in any amount)

under $50 —
$43–shoes for a child at Bet Hayeled (www.geocities.com/bhayeled/)
$40– toys for children survivors of terror for Chanukah
$38 –gas heating bill for survivor of terror
$50–for balloons and chocolate to child after operation

under $25 —
$18– for balloons for another child after operation
$4–dreidls and chocolate for child for Chanukah at a shelter for victims of domestic violence (x 30 for a group, but that was the per price)

A Very Special $22.00 Mitzvah
This is an e-mail we received from one of our other "inside contacts" in Israel. Again, details have been changed to safeguard the identity and dignity of the recipients:

> H called me to ask if I had anything to do with the flowers they received. She was so thrilled and said that she couldn't figure out who would have known about them other than me. She said they were beautiful and made them feel good. Their father was killed in a פיגוע -pigua [terrorist attack] and their mother died of one of those terrible diseases and the daughters are all in their late teens and early 20s totally on their own.

Infant Thermometers
One of Ziv Tzedakah Fund's Mitzvah heroes, Jeannie Jaybush, is working with so many poor people in Seattle it is hard to keep track of everything she does. Often, when confronted with an endless stream of possibilities and only a finite amount of Tzedakah money to give, we review her wish list with her, and we pick one or two items we can afford to purchase for her.

In the recent past she told us about the need for infant thermometers for families to have on hand at home. And then she told us a very sad story. A newborn child had been running a fever, but because the parents were illegal immigrants, they were afraid to take the infant to the emergency room. As time went on, it was clear that the child was suffering. When the visiting nurse arrived and examined the infant, the parents knew they that had to take the risk. By the time the emergency room people could take care of the child, it became clear that the child had meningitis and because of the long delay had suffered permanent damage.

This didn't have to happen. Now, our search was on for getting good prices for bulk orders of thermometers…and people to donate the money to pay for them. Ziv found contributors to cover most of the cost, then paid for the rest. Naomi Eisenberger, Ziv's Managing Director, searched for a good price and discovered that we could buy dozens at approximately $3.50 apiece. Ziv bought substantial quantities at that price. Particularly moving was the fact that the students of the early childhood department of a synagogue school donated a significant portion of the money to pay for many of the thermometers.

That was months ago.

More recently, someone remembered Jeannie's need and Naomi's quest for a good price, and the son of a good friend came through with an even better price. For $2,000, Ziv could buy approximately 780 thermometers. Adding $75.00 for shipping, that unit price came to about $2.66 a piece. For $2.66, maybe years of suffering have been avoided for hundreds of children.
For $2.66.

Infinitely More

Perhaps what I wrote in the opening paragraph is wrong. Maybe there really are infinitely more $38.00, $25.00, $10.00, and $2.66 Mitzvahs waiting to happen Out There if you seek them out. It would be nice to have more, as much, or almost as much money as God, but even if you don't, there is just so much you can do.

Just imagine — $2.66 can save a life!

How Do You Evaluate Financial Information from a Tzedakah Program So That You Can Decide to Whom to Give or Not to Give?

If you are giving to an organization, you are entitled to see a copy of its financial report. The Jewish reasoning is relatively simple. As explained in other chapters of this book, Tzedakah money is never "owned" by the donor. Rather, that portion of our income that is intended for Tzedakah is entrusted to us by God to reach appropriate recipients. If we are trustees, Jewish tradition teaches we should certainly be responsible trustees.

In a situation where you know the organization 100% top-to-bottom and backwards-and-forwards, then you may want to get a copy of the budget as a simple formality and point of reference. This is one of the wonderful advantages I have enjoyed over 30 years working with Mitzvah heroes. Since the Mitzvah heroes are absolutely trustworthy, examining the finances is relatively easy. If, however, you do not know the organization, or know them for their work but do not know their finances, ask for the "numbers". Of course, if they balk and do not want to send you any documentation, Judaism frees you from any obligation to give to them.

When you do get a copy of its finances, ask yourself, how do the figures of the non-profit generally look to you?

1. How much is the overhead? This is the essential word - overhead, costs of running the operation, salaries, fundraising expenses, publicity, office expenses, and the like.

2. How much is spent on fundraising, publicity, and similar items in relation to how much actually goes to the stated programs of the Tzedakah fund?

3. Is the financial sheet easily understandable?

4. If individuals receive salaries, do they seem reasonable to you?

5. After you have read and reviewed the financial statements, if you still have any questions, contact the organization directly. Ask yourself, were you satisfied that you received timely, straightforward, and complete answers?

Without any of the above information, you should not be giving to that fund. Today, the word "transparency" is used when referring to a non-profit's financial statements. Is it all clear, easily accessible, and without detours or obfuscating terminology and explanations? As always, if there are any doubts, you should be checking with the people behind the financial reports directly for clarification.

There is one other step you should take: Surf the internet to check if there have been any articles - positive or negative - about your potential recipients. There may be something "out there" which you need to know before you contribute. Remember, however, all information "out there" may not be accurate.

For your reference, the first mention of financial accountability is in the Bible. Concerning repairs and maintenance of the Temple in King Josiah's time, II Kings 22:7 states:

אך לא-יחשב אתם הכסף הנתן על ידם כי באמונה הם עשים

…but no accounting was done concerning the donations given, because they did their work in a trustworthy manner.

Over the course of time, Jewish tradition changed its approach. Rabbi Moshe Isserles, basing his decision on an earlier ruling, adds the following comment to a law in the 16th century Shulchan Aruch code:

הגה ומ"מ כדי שיהיו נקיים
הגה מה, ומישראל טוב להם ליתן חשבון

In any event, it is best for them [the managers of the Tzedakah fund] to give an accounting so that they stay "clean" - [as the verse states in Numbers 32:22], "…you shall be untainted both as far as God and Israel are concerned".

The following chapters will provide additional details that will help you determine how to read and understand the finances, efficiency, and accountability of organizations that you might consider supporting.

How Useful is the Internet for Your Tzedakah Research?

There is no question that the internet can be a powerful tool if you want to give your Tzedakah money away judiciously and effectively. The power of search engines, and the world-wide reach that your computer affords you, anywhere, at any time, are awesome tools. Just consider that the United States alone has approximately 1,000,000 non-profit organizations. You can easily imagine just how valuable the internet can be as a first in your search for appropriate recipients of your Tzedakah dollars.

The Internet and Individual Tzedakah Programs

Today, almost any Tzedakah project of any size has its own website which will provide background information and a basic description of what it has set out to do, and, hopefully, what it is actually doing. What you will be looking for in addition to the basic information is (1) a real, i.e., snail mail, address — a post office box listing is not sufficient, (2) a list of the board of directors as well as the employees in charge of directing the use of the Tzedakah money, (3) a copy of the budget, and (4) a way to contact the project not only by e-mail but also by phone or letter.

Furthermore, if you are interested in contributing to an organization that allows you to donate online, you will want to know how secure that area of the website is. Most Tzedakah projects in the United States use a third party service such as www.networkforgood.org to process online donations. You will need to know what percentage of your donation will be used as a processing fee. Fortunately, many of them take a very low percentage, and, as this aspect of e-philanthropy develops, competition will inevitably keep the cost to a minimum. At present, many take 3% or less. You will need to decide if this is a wise and fair use of part of your Tzedakah money. Even more, you will need to decide whether you need to add to your donation to cover the fee. If your intention is to give $200, should you be giving $206, so that the recipient receives a total of $200? This is important "Tzedakah mathematics" you need to consider as you are giving your Tzedakah.

Of the highest priority: You will want to know if either the organization itself or the donation-processing service shares your personal information with other non-profits. You need to be assured that your e-mail address and other vital statistics remain inaccessible not only to other Tzedakah programs, but also to any unauthorized person within the organization to which you may be contributing.

The Internet and "Umbrella" Websites That Monitor and Evaluate Tzedakah Programs

Several websites will provide you large databases of non-profit organizations and people doing Tikun Olam with Tzedakah money. Whatever research you do on the internet, remember that this is only an initial step in your quest to do meaningful and effective Tzedakah work. For all of the items on the next page, and others you may discover, you must review the criteria on which they base their listings, analyses, and evaluations.

For example:

1. Does the "umbrella" group only examine public documents?

2. Does it talk to or personally meet people who manage these organizations?

3. Has it spoken to people who work for these organizations, who work "on the front lines" where the actual Tikun Olam is taking place?

4. How often are the data revised and reviewed?

5. Are there some organizations and Good People making a significant impact who are not listed because they are too small to be required by law to file a tax return with the Internal Revenue Service in the United States, or the Revenue Canada? (If a non-profit's activity is less than $25,000 annually, they are not required to file.)

6. Are there still others not listed because they are not even incorporated as a non-profit but are, nevertheless, doing exceptionally important Tikun Olam work?

7. How can you find reports about family foundations which have to file a tax return, but are not required to provide a public record of their activities?

8. If one of these websites has a rating system, what is considered acceptable overhead for an organization to receive a good rating? (One such website allows 25% for fundraising and administration. In my opinion, this is much too high.)

9. And, finally, if one of these websites has a rating system of "the best", "acceptable", etc., what are the criteria for their choices? This is particularly important when you compare a Tzedakah program's ratings for more than one year. If, for example, one of them has risen or fallen in the ratings, you will need to know if you agree or disagree with how that change was determined. Sometimes the reasons do not correspond to Jewish values and/or your own personal sense of what is fair.

Following are some important websites listing North American non-profits that may be of use to you.

1. **www.ziv.org** has more than 100 programs it is involved with in North America, Israel, and other places in the world.

2. **www.guidestar.org** lists thousands of non-profit organizations, including their Form 990 which must be filed with the Internal Revenue Service.

3. **www.justgive.org** provides information similar to Guidestar's website.

4. **www.charitynavigator.org** examines the IRS 990 of 5,000 nonprofits, and then analyzes and evaluates all of the data. It also compares and contrasts similar organizations, factoring in several important variables explained on its website. In addition, it lists each organization's donor privacy policy, its mission statement, and compensation for the organization's director.

5. **www.just-tzedakah.org** lists and analyzes hundreds of Jewish organizations and groups.

For Canadians, **www.canadahelps.org** lists every non-profit in the country.

For Israeli ogranizations: In the early 1980's, Professor Eliezer Jaffe, Chairman of Hebrew University's School of Social Work, published a 656-page book called Giving Wisely: The Israel Guide to Non-Profit and Volunteer Social Services. Hundreds of organizations and programs were listed with vital information any donor would need to know before contributing money. Subsequenrly, Dr. Jaffe developed a Giving Wisely website. His work was really the first major attempt to provide potential contributors worldwide with a better, though still, preliminary understanding of how these groups were making a difference. Others have built on his model, and with the rapid advances in electronic communication, no potential donor needs to give his or her Tzedakah money without being well informed.

The more you examine both "umbrella" websites and their evaluation of non-profit organizations, and the websites of specific non-profit organizations, the more skilled you will become at interpreting what you read. If you are "not good at" finding, reading, and understanding how websites work, do not hesitate to ask someone who knows Tzedakah-and-the-internet to give you some guidance.

Ultimately, your analysis need come to include the full range of your critical abilities: Does what you read make logical and reasonable sense? Does the tone of the website make you feel comfortable, or is there something behind and beyond the words and images that is "not quite right"? Of great importance, too, is the question, "What is your overall 'gut feeling'?" It's like in computer language – WYSIWYG — what you see is what you get.

The end of the process: You will want to be in touch directly and immediately with the person you deem most appropriate within the Tzedakah organization. Then, and only then, proceed, deciding what part you want to play in this organization's Tikun Olam work.

All this having been said, remember that you will discover that amazing numbers of Tzedakah programs are absolutely wonderful and are managed with the greatest integrity.

How Much of Your Tzedakah Money Should Be Directed To Tzedakah Programs in Israel?

When you are deciding how much of your total Tzedakah budget to devote to Israel, you will need to keep in mind that there are many unique issues to be considered. A very short list includes:

1. The continued influx of immigrants coming from Ethiopia, the Former Soviet Union, Europe, America, and other parts of the world;

2. The enormous toll terrorist attacks have taken, not only on the loss of human life, but also the cost of rehabilitation of tens of thousands of physically and psychologically injured survivors;

3. The economic drain on Israel's economy due to the demands of a high defense budget,

4. The fact that, other than some select non-Jewish groups, the greatest percentage of financial support must come from the Jewish community. In addition, in recent years, North American Jews have demonstrated less commitment to Israel and its needs. This is a trend that most certainly needs to be reversed.

In light of all of these factors and many others I did not list, giving to Israel ought to be a fundamental area of your Tzedakah giving. With that understanding, you may find it helpful to consider two approaches to your Israel Tzedakah donations. The first is largely described above — Israel's unique needs. The second involves Tzedakah for individuals, groups, and Tikun Olam programs that are common to people everywhere. One of these needs is most basic — hungry people and people who live with what is called "food insecurity". This recently-coined term refers to people who, even if they have today's and tomorrow's food, still live constantly in doubt about the meals for the next day and the day after that. Additional common social needs include: people who are living on the financial edge, children who have an educational experience that could be 100% or 200% better if the resources were available, health care needs, etc. The list is very long. You yourself, could easily name another dozen.

There is a relatively simple technique to help you consider this second category, i.e., "common" needs. While you are deciding how to use your Tzedakah money, make a habit of putting the word "Israel" before the general category. For example, you may be particularly concerned about people who have Alzheimer's. You could give to Alzheimer's programs in North America, but by making the mental note, "Israel - Alzheimer's", you may also consider using Tzedakah money for effective programs in Israel that need your support. The same would be true, for example, for "at-risk children"–"Israel-at-risk children", "people with special needs"–"Israel - people with special needs", and "Elders living with dignity"–"Israel - Elders living with dignity". www.ziv.org will be a useful website for exploring both types of needs in Israel - the unique and the common.

How you ultimately decide which percentage of your Tzedakah money goes to Israel's unique or common needs, is, of course, your personal decision. Nevertheless, I personally believe that giving significant percentages of your Tzedakah money to Israel should be a major component of every Jewish person's financial commitment.

The same rules apply to giving overseas as to giving locally. But, the information that you require can be much more difficult to attain, and very difficult to understand. There are issues of seeing the place, meeting the key person on the job there (your Mitzvah hero), getting the financial information, understanding it both for language (if it is not in English) and for local cultural nuances, and then being able to decide what to do.

For example, you heard great things about an organization in Israel that is working with Ethiopian immigrants there. Even if you've been there and even if you have met the Mitzvah hero, you still need a way to assess the financial status and spending of the organization. It is not sufficient that your best friend's aunt went there and loves the place. You need to make your own decisions based on your own information.

It is always best to have assistance, using the same principles for giving away money. Find someone you trust completely (either locally or overseas) and be sure that this person has the ability, knowledge and experience to be your eyes and ears. This person becomes your agent and will report back to you with the appropriate information.

Do not be discouraged from giving Tzedakah money to places in Israel, but do not give blindly either.

What is an "American Friends of" organization?

Many overseas non-profits, particularly those in Israel, need a way for American citizens to get a tax break when making a donation. American law is clear that an American citizen can only get a tax break when donating to a legal American non-profit–called a 501(c)(3). An Israeli non-profit does not qualify.

So, they will set up a legal organization in the USA for tax deductible purposes, called the American Friends of 'x', thereby allowing American citizens to donate legally and get a tax deduction. (This is often a very important part of giving - for every dollar you donate to a recognized non-profit, you reduce your tax paid. True, you don't get to keep the money, but at least it is better spent by it going to a non-profit!)

All "American Friends of" organizations must abide by American law and file the appropriate papers (called a 990) at the end of the year. This "American Friends of" organization is its own entity. That is, it has income, expenses, and needs to be checked out by itself, apart from its Israeli counterpart. And, of course, the Israeli counterpart also needs to be checked out very carefully.

For example, you give $100 to the American Friends of Israeli "X". The American Friends organization has expenses of 14%, so, $86 of your total will be then passed on the the actual non-profit in Israel. BUT, then, the Israeli organization has expenses too, of course, and let's say they spend 12% on overhead. So, another $10+ dollars of your donation has now gone to overhead, leaving $75 and change to go to the actual program. And be aware that some American Friends organizations operate very efficiently and the Israeli non-profit does not, or vice-versa. Again, both need to be checked out carefully.

Also, the websites Charity Navigator and Guidestar only will show information about the American Friends organizations and will show nothing about the Israeli counterparts.

Should You Use Some of Your Tzedakah Money to Pay for Operating Expenses and Other Overhead Needs?

At certain times, yes.

For many worthy Tikun Olam programs and Mitzvah heroes and their work, the greatest worry is finding the money to allow them to continue to function. For example, if they have recently established their program, anticipated and unanticipated start-up costs can be a serious impediment to the program's stability. In addition, sometimes the work they are doing has found a way to solve a problem more broadly, profoundly, and efficiently than any other existing structure. Even with the best planning, the demand for their Mitzvah work may have grown rapidly. Occasionally, it grows so quickly and so unexpectedly, there was no way anyone could have anticipated the demand. They become overwhelmed by requests from all quarters and need to expand just to keep pace with the demand for their services.

Even though most donors would prefer to actually pay for a scholarship "to send a kid to camp", or to buy food for people who are hungry, it is important to consider that Mitzvah heroes and Tikun Olam programs could do their work much more effectively by upgrading their computers, or adding a staff member to assume administrative responsibilities that would free the World Changers to do what they do best. Mitzvah heroes need time to devote their energies to the lives of others, offering them opportunities, hope, and life-saving services. And, they need to do it in their own unique way. In situations such as these, it would be proper —even recommended — to use some of your Tzedakah money to pay for the printing of brochures, rent, insurance, tax preparation costs, or similar overhead items. Your Tzedakah "investment" will extend the reach of the Tikun Olam program many times over in two ways: (1) The program will gain greater support and reach more people in need, and (2) as noted above, it will free those doing the Tikun Olam work to do what they do best, i.e., front-line Repairing the World.

It is, of course, your own choice how you want to balance your contributions for overhead with direct, immediate Tikun Olam. Whatever your final decision, it is important to keep in mind that, at certain times, and for certain Mitzvah heroes and projects, you should consider both to be legitimate uses of your Tzedakah money.

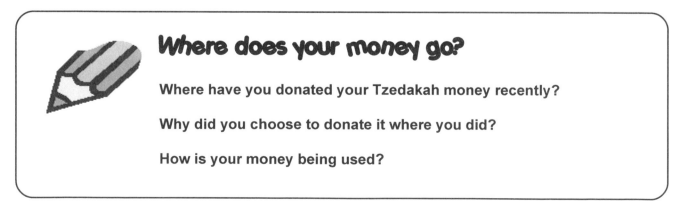

Where does your money go?

Where have you donated your Tzedakah money recently?

Why did you choose to donate it where you did?

How is your money being used?

What if a Tzedakah Organization
(1) Has Slick Publicity
(2) Keeps Sending You Mail, or
(3) Gives or Sells Your Name to Other Tzedakah Organizations Without Your Express Consent?

In each of the three cases noted above, you may feel reluctant to donate. I will address each separately, but as you read my comments and consider whether or not to continue to send money, remember that there may be groups other than these that are doing equally fine or better work in the specific "field" of Tikun Olam that interests you:

1. Slick publicity: Included in this category is an organization that has a very sophisticated website, and/or a highly professional-quality video/DVD. In most cases, you will be hesitant to donate because you believe that it is spending far too much money on overhead. You are more than likely correct, but there is one exception — when someone who believes in the Tikun Olam work of the group has created the publicity for free, at cost, or at a greatly reduced price. Check to see if such a notice appears anywhere on the publicity. If not, and, if you really believe in the organization's work, contact the person in charge and ask for the details. If he or she says that the work was done for free or at a significant discount, you may want to suggest that the group state that explicitly. If it was not done for free, at cost, or at a reasonably reduced price, politely convey your dissatisfaction, and suggest the group change its policy, as you would be reluctant to continue to donate if it is spending so much money on publicity and fundraising.

2. Mail overload: Mass mailing is a decades-old industry which has been studied and analyzed from every angle. While mass mailings serve an important function for many businesses, individuals, and Tzedakah organizations ("kosher" and otherwise), be aware that a 3% return rate is considered high for many types of these mailings. In and of itself, mass mailings handled by professional mailing houses are not "bad", though I am generally opposed to them in the Tzedakah world. Again, if this is an organization that meets so many other good criteria, you will want to (1) contact the person in charge and ask how much was spent on the mailing(s) compared to how much Tzedakah money was actually received, and (2) you may ask to be removed from the mailing list, since you feel that you are being "overwhelmed" by the mail, and it is giving you second thoughts about the good work the organization is doing. You may add that you feel that, as "effective" as mass mailing may be for raising funds, you believe it is ultimately counterproductive. It may cause others to stop giving not only to this organization's Mitzvah work, but also to Tzedakah in general.

3. Giving or selling your name to other organizations without your express consent: In no uncertain terms, this is unethical Jewishly and a severe abuse of the donor. At this point, it is not enough to tell the group that you want to be dropped from the mailing list. You will also want to inform them — preferably by phone, or if possible, face-to-face — that you believe this is a violation of Jewish ethics.

Deciding Where to Give: Mail and Phone Solicitations

From the explanations given elsewhere in this book, it should be clear that, unless the mail solicitation includes satisfactory financial information, you have no obligation to give. In fact, Maimonides and subsequent Jewish legal rulings statethat you should not be giving to that organization. With solicitations over the phone, your procedure should be similar and relatively simple: Ask the solicitor to mail or e-mail you the organization's financial reports. If the organization does not, then your obligation to give ends there. If it does, and you are satisfied with what you learn about their fiscal responsibility, then you can decide whether or not you want to contribute.

A true story:

One rabbi was so overwhelmed with mail solicitations, he felt he needed to contact me. He sent me a seven-page list of all the organizations asking for money, and a check for Ziv Tzedakah Fund, the non-profit organization I founded. As a rabbi, he naturally had many other responsibilities, and while he had the time to do some research on his own, he simply did not have enough time to investigate responsibly. Since he knew that there were several on his list that I trusted, he asked me to distribute his Tzedakah money as I deemed appropriate.

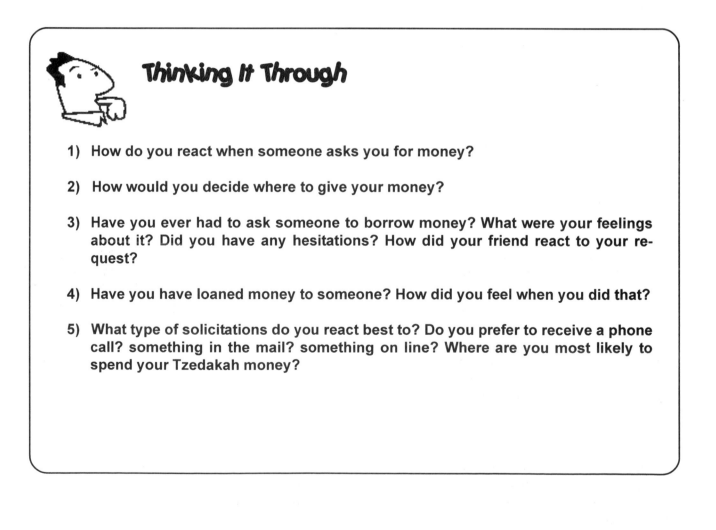

Thinking It Through

1) How do you react when someone asks you for money?

2) How would you decide where to give your money?

3) Have you ever had to ask someone to borrow money? What were your feelings about it? Did you have any hesitations? How did your friend react to your request?

4) Have you have loaned money to someone? How did you feel when you did that?

5) What type of solicitations do you react best to? Do you prefer to receive a phone call? something in the mail? something on line? Where are you most likely to spend your Tzedakah money?

What If Someone Is Hungry?

The classic Jewish text concerning this question is as follows:

ורב יהודה אמר: בודקין לכסות ואין בודקין למזונות

Rav Yehuda said,
We may investigate when someone asks for clothing;
but we do not investigate when the need is for food.

(Talmud Bava Batra 9a)

Rav Yehuda's statement, incorporated in the codes of Jewish Law, is intended for individuals literally asking for food in your presence. In that kind of a situation, there is no way of knowing if a delay might cause severe complications or even death.

A Talmudic story (Ta'anit 21a) about Nachum Ish Gamzu is generally referred to as proof. He was riding on a donkey leading a second donkey laden with food supplies.

A man approached and said, "Rabbi, feed me." Nachum replied, "Wait until I unload [the food] from the donkey's saddlebags."

By the time he had begun to get the food, the man had died.

This is an extreme case, but the truth is that you can never know how close another person is to dying of starvation.

Again, this text applies to someone who is directly asking for food. The issue is the very thin line between a human being who is still alive and שעת יציאת הנשמה, the very moment of death, when it is too late to do anything.

A conversation with a doctor or nurse will help you focus on the extreme urgency of that unique moment.

"Rabbi Chana bar Chanila'i had sixty bakers in his house day and night, baking for anyone who needed bread. He would leave his hand in his pocket so that (by the immediacy and naturalness of handing money to him or her) a poor person who came to ask would not feel humiliated. His doors were open to all four directions, and whoever came in hungry would leave satisfied. Furthermore, in times when food was scarce, he would leave wheat and barley outside the door, so that anyone who was too embarrassed to come and take in the daytime could come unnoticed and take a night."

(Talmud Berachot 58b)

We are reminded of the stories of Abraham and Job, both of whom had their tents open to the four directors. Both took the initiative to be on the look-out to make Tzedakah part of their lives, and Rabbi Chana bar Chanila'i did the same—as well as adding many insights into the prevention of Bushah. A split-second act—taking a hand and putting it into the pocket to take money out—might have caused shame to the person in need—and this Rabbi wished to avoid that at all costs.

Should You Give to People in The Street?

"A story is told of Binyamin HaTzaddik, who was the supervisor of the community's Tzedakah-funds. Once, when food was scarce, a woman came to him and said 'Rabbi, feed me!' He replied, 'I swear that there is nothing in the Tzedakah-fund.' She said, 'If you do not feed me, a woman and her seven children will die.' So he fed her from his own money." (Talmud Bava Batra 11a)

This story simply states the principal: When nothing can be done, something can still be done. Even though his official responsibilities ended when the communal funds were exhausted, Binyamin's obligations as a Jew demanded some deliberate action. Something had to be done and Binyamin rose to the occasion.

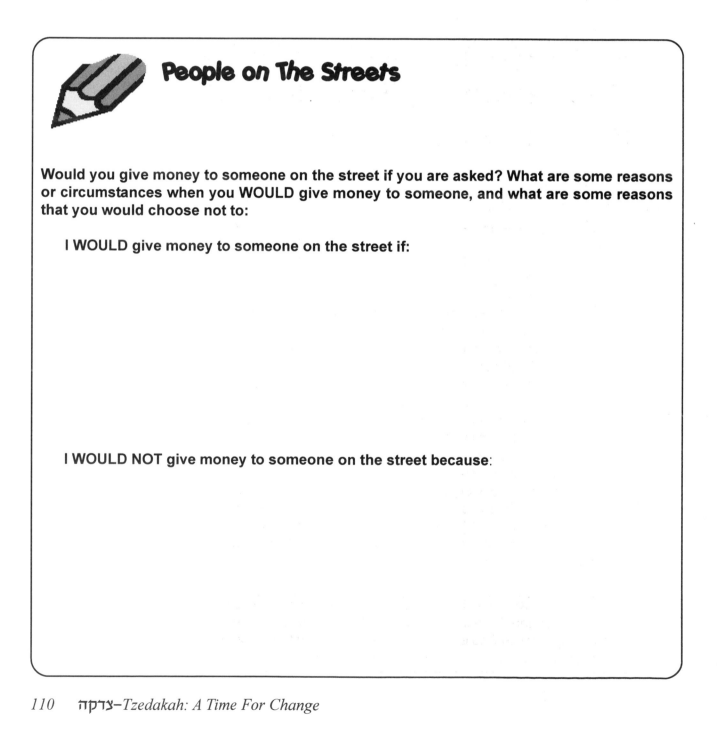

People on The Streets

Would you give money to someone on the street if you are asked? What are some reasons or circumstances when you WOULD give money to someone, and what are some reasons that you would choose not to:

I WOULD give money to someone on the street if:

I WOULD NOT give money to someone on the street because:

Should you give to people on the street?

Some reasons why you might choose not to give are:

1. What if they just use it to buy alcohol or drugs?

2. As I walk to work, what if there are so many of them, I couldn't possibly provide for all of them?

3. If I keep giving to them, won't this strain my Tzedakah budget to the limit?

4. Wouldn't it be better to buy them a meal?

Brother, Can You Spare a Dime: The Treatement of Beggars According to Jewish Tradition

By Arthur Kurzweil*

In my neighborhood in Manhattan there is hardly a day when I am not approached by an individual who asks me for spare change, a quarter, a subway token, or some other request of similar nature. These individuals (whom I will call "beggars" from this point on, though I am aware that this label is narrow and therefore unfair to use to describe a human being) come in various forms:

1. Some are bag ladies, dragging the sum-total of their worldly possessions with them in numerous shopping bags.
2. Some are "street people" who most probably live on the street, in the subway, or other public places.
3. Some are idle welfare recipients who would strike you as people who would probably be able to get some kind of job.
4. Some are alcoholics, constantly with bottle in hand or nearby.
5. Some are obvious drug addicts.
6. Some show no immediately-apparent reason to be asking for anything as they are well-dressed, groomed, etc.
7. They are of all ages (literally from 8 to 80).
8. They are both men and women.
9. They are usually black or Hispanic (in my neighborhood, but in Greenwich Village however, where I often walk, they are mostly white and sometimes Jewish).
10. 99 times out of 100 they are non-threatening (though I am a male and I imagine that if I were a woman I would have a significantly different perspective on this item.)

(Editor's Note: Arthur Kurzweil has graciously granted his permission to reprint excerpts of this article. The article appears here from pages 111-120. The original purpose of this article was to serve as a model for text study in English. Since this book is devoted to Tzedakah, I have not included the additional bibliographic information that accompanied the original article.)

Though the organized Jewish community has gotten the Mitzvah of giving Tzedakah down to a virtual science, and though I have also been a member of an alternative form of giving Tzedakah for 4 years (a "Tzedakah collective;" see The *Third Jewish Catalog*, p. 31, Jewish Publication Society, 1980), I was confused as to what I should do about beggars I meet almost daily.   My habit regarding beggars was inconsistent:

1. Sometimes I gave nothing, both in one given day as well as for occasional blocks of time
2. Sometimes I'd get into a giving mood and give to beggars in a flurry of giving over a period of time
3. Sometimes I'd get into angry moods over the issue and never give a penny, thinking that they "ought to get a job" or "ought to go on welfare."
4. Sometimes I'd give consistently though selectively to people I decided were worthy recipients (the standards for that decision might be impossible for me to even document).
5. Sometimes I'd give enthusiastically to a familiar beggar, only to ignore the person the next day or week.

There were other inconsistencies as well, but those five listed above are enough to indicate that my thinking on the subject was, as I said, confused. But more than confused, I was troubled by it. A question loomed in my mind: What should my attitude toward beggars be? And secondly: Did Jewish tradition have anything to teach me on the subject?

 ## What should my attitude be?

When approaching the first question of "What should my attitude toward beggars be?" the first step is to sit down and brainstorm all of the questions that you can come up with relating to your own personal dilemmas. For example, "Do Jews give to beggars?", "What if they smell badly?", "What if I'm not in the mood to be friendly?"

How many other questions can you come up with?

The following are the results of my own exploration of those two questions. First, though, I would like to make a few things clear regarding my research:

1. I am not a Talmudic scholar.
2. I do not have a working knowledge of Hebrew or Aramaic, so all of the sources I have consulted are in English.
3. Every source quoted comes from my home library.

This third point is made for two reasons. First, I want to stress that the sources I have checked are limited. But secondly, I want to indicate that quite a bit of research of this kind can be productive by using readily available sources - again - in English.

My approach to the first question of "What should my attitude toward beggars be?" was to first sit down and list all of the question I could possibly think of relating to my own personal dilemmas in regard to the subject. I came up with 15 questions:

1. Do Jews give to beggars? (Is there precedent for my giving to beggars - as a Jew who wants to fulfill the Mitzvah of Tzedakah).
2. What if they are fakes or frauds? (How many times I have wondered whether they are making more than me!)
3. What if they are nasty or otherwise offensive in looks, smell, etc.?
4. What if I fell I simply can't afford to give to beggars (having already given through other means)?
5. Aren't there better causes to give to than these people?
6. Shouldn't these beggars be supported by official or organized agencies?
7. Shouldn't I just ignore these people?
8. What if I am in a rush? (In my hectic life I barely have time to stop and negotiate a quarter for a "wino.")
9. What if they aren't Jewish? (Should my Tzedakah priorities go to worthy Jewish causes exclusively?)
10. What if I have no money on me, or no spare change?
11. If I do give, how should I treat these people? What should I say to them?
12. What if I see the same people every day? (They'll get to know me as an easy sucker.)
13. What if I've give to a few beggars in one day? (Is there a limit to this?)
14. If they ask for money, perhaps I should go buy them a cup of coffee instead. After all, they will probably spend it on booze anyway!
15. Finally, if I do give to beggars, how much should I give?

The fifteen questions seemed to cover just about every possible question or issue I could possibly come up with regarding beggars. Interestingly, I noticed that the first 10 questions raised objections to giving to beggars while the last 5 seems to admit defeat, wondering just how and what to give if I must. In all, my questions reflected a resistance to giving to beggars - while my eagerness to do research on the subject balanced that resistance.

While I was apparently born with an interest in research, I grew up in a home where my parents were constantly asking questions and forever referring to the family encyclopedia. Adding that to my training as a librarian, I find it rather easy to find simple answers to simple (and not so simple) questions. But I am also convinced that without any training - other than learning a few principles and doing a minimum of creative thinking - anyone can master the art of elementary research....

My first question when looking for insight into the Jewish view of beggars is to figure out what key words would help me to "dig out" the material. With some creativity and a lot of trial and error I found that beggars would appear under the following topics:

1. beggars
2. poor
3. charity

"Tzedakah" was never a category; it was always translated as "charity" in the indexes. I spent a frantic and exciting few days running up and down my shelves, grabbing books which I thought might have items under these three headings. In a great number of cases I was quite successful. I read an enormous amount, copying lines, passages, quotes, and paragraphs. If a secondary source (such as a Jewish quotation dictionary) gave me a Talmudic passage, I was able to go to the Talmud itself - in English of course, and see it a little closer to the original - as well as the context in which it appeared. Often, by going to the "original" I was able to find more material on the subject which the secondary source left out. I was also able to compare translations (and when there were significant conflicts between translations I'd be on the phone to Danny Siegel once again for a glimpse - through his eyes - at the original original!)

After going through every book in my home library, I put each source on beggars which I had found on separate note cards. By the end I had about 60 cards! That is, 60 different times when some source added to my knowledge of how Jewish tradition views beggars. In the process, I read a great deal, learned more than I ever hoped to, and most remarkably I felt that I had a significant insight into the subject at hand.

Perhaps the most amazing result of my search on this subject (which might come as a surprise to some and none at all to others) is that each of my 15 questions about beggars was dealt with by one or more of the sources I discovered. Our tradition is amazing: what I would have thought was a quite contemporary question - such as what do you do if you think the beggar is a fake? - is dealt with in ancient texts....Here are my fifteen questions and the material I found which corresponds to each one:

1. DO JEWS GIVE TO BEGGARS?

> Our Rabbis taught: If an orphan boy and an orphan girl applied for maintenance, the girl orphan is to be maintained first and the boy orphan afterwards, because it is not unusual for a man to go begging, but it is unusual for a woman to do so.

> (Ketubot 67a)

(The passage is a bit sexist - reflecting the times in which it was written, of course. But I put it here, and put it first to indicate that it is sometimes difficult to "swallow" everything one comes across in the texts....

> R. Hiyya advised his wife, "When a poor man come to the door, give him food so that the same may be done to your children." She exclaimed, "You are cursing them (by suggesting that they may become beggars)! But R. Hiyya replied, "There is a wheel which revolves in this world."

> (Shabbat 151b)

(The "R." before a person's name denotes "Rabbi.")

> R. Abun said: The poor man stands at your door, and the Holy One, blessed be He, stands at his right hand. If you give unto him, He who stands at his right hand will bless

you, but if not, He will exact punishment from you, as it is said, "Because He standeth at the right hand of the needy." (Psalm 109:31)

(Midrash Ruth V:9)

R. Isaac said, "He who gives a coin to a poor man is rewarded with six blessings. but he who encourages him with friendly words is rewarded with eleven."

(Talmud Bava Batra 9a)

Question #1 is therefore answered. There is no question but that it is within the Jewish tradition to give to beggars. But we have 14 questions remaining, each of which tries to obtain a better understanding of the complexities of the whole issue.

2. WHAT IF THEY ARE FAKES OR FRAUDS?

Our Rabbis taught: If a man pretends to have a blind eye, a swollen belly or a shrunken leg, he will not pass out from this world before actually coming into such a condition. I a man accepts charity and is not in need of it, his end will be that he will not pass out of the world before he comes to such a condition.

(Ketubot 68a)

R. Akiva said, He who takes even a penny from charity when he needs it not will not die before he requires the help of man. He said, He who binds rags on his eyes or on his loins and says, "Give to the blind man," or "Give to the man who is smitten with boils," will end by having good cause to utter this cry.

(Mishnah Avos d'R. Natan I,iii,8a)

He who needs not and takes will not reach old age and die before he will really need help from others . . . He who is not lame or blind but pretends to be so, will not reach old age and die before he becomes really blind and lame.

(Jerusalem Talmud, Pe'ah 8:9)

If anyone is not in need of relief and yet receives it by deceiving the public, he will not die of old age before becoming a public charge. Such a person is included in the Biblical utterance: "A curse on him who relies on man." (Jer. 17:5)

(Rambam, Mishneh Torah"Gifts to Poor People" 10:19)

(These first 4 items agree and even seem to quote from each other. The message is clear, but it still doesn't help us. Should we give to the fakers? All we know so far is that they'll be punished for faking. Onward:)

R. Eleazar said: Come let us be grateful to the rogues for if not for them we (who do not always respond to every appeal for charity) would have been sinning every day.

(Talmud Ketubot 68a)

R. Hanina was wont to send a poor man four zuzim every Friday. Once he sent them by his wife, who reported on her return that the man was not in need. "What did you see?" said the Rabbi. "I heard how he was asked, 'Would he use the silver outfit or the gold outfit.'" Then R. Hanina said, This is what R. Eleazar said: We must be grateful to the deceivers, for were it not for them, we might sin every day.

(Talmud Ketubot 68a)

(In other words, the fakers keep us in the habit of giving.)

A beggar once came to the city of Kovna and collected a large sum of money from the residents. The people of the town soon found out that he was an impostor; he really was a wealthy man. The city council wanted to make an ordinance prohibiting beggars from coming to Kovna to collect money. When R. Yitzchok Elchonon Specter, the Rabbi of Kovna, heard about the proposed ordinance, he came before the council and requested permission to speak. He told them that although he sympathized with them, he had an objection to raise. "Who deceived you, a needy person or a wealthy person? It was a wealthy person feigning poverty. If you want to make an ordinance, it should be to ban wealthy persons from collecting alms. But why make a ban against needy beggars?"

(Ethics from Sinai, III, p. 121)

Rabbi Chayim of Sanz had this to say about fraudulent charity collectors: "The merit of charity is so great that I am happy to give to 100 beggars even if only one might actually be needy. Some people, however, act as if they are exempt from giving charity to 100 beggars in the event that one might be a fraud."

(Darkai Chayim (1962), p. 137)

(The last quote, for the Sanzer Rebbe Chayim Halberstam, who was the teacher of my great-great-great grandfather, Chayim Joseph Gottlieb, the Stropkover Rebbe, seems to sum up question #2 clearly: Don't let the frauds stop you from giving. And as the earlier sources quoted point out: the frauds will get theirs!)

3. WHAT IF THEY ARE NASTY OR OTHERWISE OFFENSIVE?

The Chofetz Chayim's son wrote that his father was particularly careful not to hurt the feelings of beggars, although sometimes these unfortunate people say things that could arouse one's anger.

(Michtevai Chofetz Chayim (1953)
(Dugmah Midarkai Avi, p. 38)

Rabbi Shmelke of Nicholsburg said, "When a poor man asks you for aid, do not use his faults as an excuse for not helping him. For then God will look for your offenses, and He is sure to find many of them. Keep in mind that the poor man's transgressions have been atoned for by his poverty while yours still remain with you.

(Fun Unzer Alter Otzer, II, p. 99)

(The last quote, couple with the first one, is somewhat helpful when dealing with the question of the alcoholic who asks for money. In some ways, the suffering he is undergoing is "punishment" enough. My denying him money "because he'd only use it for booze" is not helping anyone.)

4. WHAT IF I FEEL I SIMPLY CAN'T AFFORD TO GIVE TO BEGGARS?

To him who has the means and refuses the need, the Holy One says: Bear in mind, fortune is a wheel!

(Nahman, Tanhuma, Mishpatim #8)

Even a poor man, a subject of charity, should give charity.

(Talmud Gittin 7b)

5. AREN'T THERE ANY BETTER CAUSES TO GIVE TO THAN TO THESE PEOPLE?

While it is commendable to aid students of the Torah more than commoners, the Jewish law knows no such distinction. The latter must also be aided.

(Nachman of Bratslave quoted in Hasidic Anthology)

(This "excuse" noted below is a familiar one to me. How often I have passed by a beggar thinking: I gave to Oxfam International - The World Hunger Organization. The irony is to obvious to explain!)

6. SHOULDN'T THESE BEGGARS BE SUPPORTED BY OFFICIAL OR ORGANIZED AGENCIES?

In answer to an enquiry from a community, overburdened with beggars, Solomon b. Adret ruled that although, "the poor are everywhere supported from the communal chest, if they wish in addition to beg from door to door they may do so, and each should give according to his understanding and desire."

(Responsa, pt. 3, #380)

7. SHOULDN'T I JUST IGNORE THESE PEOPLE?

R. Joshua b. Korkha said, "Anyone who shuts his eye against charity is like one who worships idols."

(Talmud Ketubot 68a also Jerusalem Talmud, Peah 4:20)

R. Joshua b. Korkha said, "He who closes his eyes to a request for charity is considered as one who worships idols."

(Talmud Bava Batra 10a)

(The same person with the same thought, in two different locations in the Talmud)

A blind beggar accosted two men walking on the road. One of the travelers gave him a coin, but the other gave him nothing. That Angel of Death approached them and said: "He who gave to the beggar need have no fear of me for 50 years, but the other shall speedily die."
"May I not return and give charity to the beggar?" asked the condemned man.
"No," replied the Angel of Death. "A boat is examined for holes and cracks before departure, not when it is already at sea."

(Midrash in Me'il Zedakah)

If one noticed a poor man asking for something and ignored him, and failed to give Tzedakah, he has broken a prohibitive command, as it is written: Do not harden your heart and shut your hand against your needy brother. (Deut. 17:7)

(Rambam, Mishneh Torah"Gifts to Poor People" 7:2)

Rabbi Itzikel of Kalish was known for his kindness for everyone. Once a non-Jewish beggar asked the Rabbi's wife for some bread. At the moment she had only a full loaf, newly baked, and she disliked cutting it lest it become dry. But the Rabbi enjoined her to give the beggar a portion of this bread. A few years later, the Rabbi was traveling through the Carpathian Mountains toward Hungary. On the way brigands captured him and his companions, and brought them to their chieftain. The latter recognized the Rabbi as his benefactor when he came begging at his door. He freed Rabbi Itzikel and restored to him his possessions.

(Or ha-Meir (Lemberg, 1926), p. 15)

(The preceeding is a strange story for a few reasons. First, the lesson is clearly not: give to beggars because they might become crooks and rob you. Second, like too many stories, the hero is the Rabbi, while the insensitive one is the wife. Thirdly, the beggar is a non-Jew. Despite all this, the moral message still manages to sneak through: don't ignore beggars.)

> Rabbi Aharon Kotler once gave alms twice to the same beggar, upon entering and leaving the synagogue. He was afraid that someone noticing him pass the second time without giving might assume that he had reason not to give to this particular beggar.
>
> (R. Shaul Kagan in Jewish Observer, 5/73)

8. WHAT IF I AM IN A RUSH?

(The following story, from the Talmud, is one of the most vivid and powerful ones I've encountered. Every detail is radically unsettling.)

> It is related of Nahum of Gamzu that he was blind in both his eyes, his two hands and legs were amputated, and his whole body was covered with boils and he was lying in a dilapidated house on a bed the feet of which were standing in bowls of water to prevent the ants from crawling on to him. On one occasion his disciples desired to remove the bed and then clear the things out of the house, but he said to them, "My children, first clear out the things from the house and then remove my bed for I am confident that so long as I am in the house it will not collapse." They first cleared out the things and then removed the bed and the house immediately collapsed. Thereupon his disciples said to him, "Master, since you are wholly righteous, why has all this befallen you?" and he replied, "I have brought it all upon myself. Once I was journeying on the road and was making for the house of my father-in-law and I had with me three asses, one laden with food, one with drink, and one with all kinds of dainties, when a poor man met me and stopped me on the road and said to me, 'Master, give me something to eat.' I replied to him, 'Wait until I have unloaded something from the ass; I had hardly managed to unload something from the ass when the man died (from hunger). I then went and laid myself upon him and exclaimed, 'May my eyes which had no pity upon your eyes become blind, may my hands with had no pity on your hands be cut off, may my legs which had no pity upon your legs be amputated,' and my mind was not at rest until I added, 'may my whole body be covered with boils.'" Thereupon his pupils exclaimed, "Alas that we see you in such a sore plight." To this he replied, "Woe would it be to me if you did not see me in such a sore plight."
>
> (Talmud Ta'anit 21a)

9. WHAT IF THEY AREN'T JEWISH?

(The irony of this question is that when I was in Israel and when I met poor Jewish beggars in Eastern Europe, I never questioned the idea of giving to them. My own prejudices became crystal clear with this question!)

> A Jew should give charity to poor non-Jews.
>
> (Rambam, Mishneh Torah "Gifts to Poor People" 7:7)

> Poor Gentiles should be supported along with poor Jews; the Gentile sick should be visited along with the Jewish sick; and their dead should be buried along with the Jewish dead, in order to further peaceful relations.
>
> (Talmud Gittin 61a)

(These last two items reflect a limitation on my part. In my reading I know that there are long discussions as to the true meaning and nature of the phrase "peaceful relations." On the surface it sounds as if we must do it not because it's right but for peace. The matter is much more complicated than that and is one that I do not have the ability to examine at this point. This is clearly one of the drawbacks of my own limited background.)

10. WHAT IF I HAVE NO MONEY ON ME OR NO SPARE CHANGE?

If a poor man requests money from you and you have nothing to give him, speak to him consolingly.

(Rambam, Mishneh Torah "Gifts to Poor People" 10:5)

If the poor man stretches out his hand and he has nothing to give him, he should not scold and raise his voice to him, but he should speak gently to him and show him his goodness of heart; namely that he wishes to give him something but cannot.

(Shulchan Aruch, Yoreh De'ah, 249:3-5)

Walking one day in Jerusalem, Rabbi Aharon Kotler turned around, ran after a beggar, and gave him some coins. Rabbi Kotler explained that several years previously, the same beggar had approached him for alms, but he was carrying no money. Spotting that beggar now, he hastened to make up for lost opportunity, and gave him a double amount.

(R. Shaul Kagan, Jewish Observer, 5/73)

11. IF I DO GIVE, HOW SHOULD I TREAT THESE PEOPLE? WHAT SHOULD I SAY? HOW SHOULD I APPROACH THEM?

Rabbi Chana bar Chanila'i . . . would leave his hand in his pocket so that (by the immediacy and naturalness of handing him money) a poor person who came to ask would not feel humiliated.

(Talmud Brachot 58b)

R. Eleazar stated, The reward of charity depends entirely upon the extent of kindness in it.

(Talmud Sukkah 49b)

Anyone who gives Tzedakah in a surly manner and with a gloomy face completely nullifies the merit of his own deed, even if he gives him a thousand gold pieces. He should rather give him cheerfully and gladly, while sympathizing with him who is in trouble, as it is written, "Did I not weep for him whose day was hard? Was not my soul grieved for the poor?" (Job 30:25)

(Rambam, Mishneh Torah "Gifts to Poor People" 10:4)

12. WHAT IF I SEE THE SAME PEOPLE EVERY DAY? WON'T THEY GET TO KNOW ME AS A SUCKER?

Though you may have given already, give yet again even a hundred times, for it says, "Give, yea, give thou shalt . . ." (Deut. 15:10-11)
[n.b. the repetition of the word for "give" teaches that the action is to be repeated]

(Sifre Deut., Re'eh, 116)

13. WHAT IF I ALREADY GAVE TO A FEW BEGGARS IN ONE DAY?

If you have given a 'perutah' to a man in the morning, and there comes to you in the evening another poor man asking for alms, give to him also . . .

(Mishnah Avot d'R. Natan 19b)

14. IF THEY ASK FOR MONEY, PERHAPS I SHOULD BUY THEM A CUP OF COFFEE INSTEAD?

Nehemiah of Sihin met a man in Jerusalem who said to him, "Give me that chicken you are carrying." Nehemiah said, "Here is its value in money." The man went and bought some meat and ate it and died. Then Nehemiah said, "Come and bemoan the man whom Nehemiah has killed."

(Jerusalem Talmud, Pe'ah, VIII: 9,21b)

(In this example, the case was reversed: the person wanted an item of food rather than money. But the point is the same: don't decide what is best for the beggar.)

15. HOW MUCH SHOULD I GIVE?

There was a poor man who begged from door to door, and R. Papa paid no attention to him. R. Samma, the son of R. Yiba, said to R. Papa, "If you pay no attention to him, then no one will, and he may starve to death." But is there not a baraita which tells us that if a man begs from door to door, the community has nothing to do with him? "The baraita is simply trying to tell us that he should not be given a large amount, but a small contribution should be made."
[n.b. a "baraita" is an alternative to the generally agreed upon interpretation of a matter]

(Talmud Bava Batra 9a)

A penny here and a penny there adds up to a great sum.

(Nachman of Bratslav, quoted in Hasidic Anthology)

A pauper who begs from house to house should be given only a small sum.

(Shulchan Aruch, Yoreh De'ah, 250: 1-5)

It is forbidden to turn away a poor man entirely empty-handed. Let him give something, if only a fig, for it is written, "Oh, let not the oppressed return ashamed." (Psalm 74:21)

(R. Moshe Isserles note on Shulchan Aruch, Yoreh De'ah, 249: 3-5)

A poor man who goes begging should not be given a large donation, but a small one. One must never turn a poor man away empty-handed, even if you give him a dry fig."

(Rambam, Mishneh Torah "Gifts to Poor People" 7:7)

A penny for the poor will obtain a view of the Shekhinah.

(Dosetai b Yannai in Talmud Bava Batra 10a)

R Eleazar used to give a coin to a poor man and straightaway say a prayer because, he said, it is written, "I in righteousness shall behold thy face."

(Talmud Bava Batra 10a)

As tiny scales join to form a strong coat of mail, so little donations combine to form a large total of good.

(Talmud Bava Batra 9b)

Just as in a garment every thread unites with the rest to form a whole garment, so every penny given to charity unites with the rest to form a large sum.

(Talmud Bava Batra 9b)

The message seems clear; don't ignore the beggar, don't treat him or her with anything but kindness, don't find excuses as to why not to give. Rather, give to everyone, regardless of who he or she is, but just give a little.

R. Assi observed: Tzedakah is as important as all the other commandments put together.

(Talmud Bava Batra 9a)

Who Benefits More-- The Giver or the Recipient?

תני בש, ר, יהושע
יותר ממה שבעל הבית עושה עם העני
העני עושה עם בעל הבית

It was taught in the name of Rabbi Yehoshua:
The poor person [standing at the door] does more for the householder
than the householder does for the poor person.

(Leviticus Rabba (Margoliot Edition) 34:8)

Because of the very nature of Tzedakah, there are those who say that the giver gets more out of the act of Tzedakah than the recipient. People who are engaged in Tikun Olam clearly benefit in many ways. Just a few of the benefits: You feel good, you feel a sense of accomplishment, and you acquire a sense of greater meaning in your life. This last glorious feeling was expressed nearly 2,000 years ago when Ben Azzai taught that, "ששכר מצוה מצוה-The reward for a Mitzvah is the Mitzvah itself." (Pirkay Avot 4:2) In and of themselves, Mitzvahs have the power to take a person into higher realms of meaning. Tzedakah most assuredly is one of the Mitzvahs that has that power...even if you have used your money to do something as "un-sublime" as paying the salary of a nurse's aide who changes diapers on adults who are no longer capable of caring for themselves.

All that said, I would humbly take issue with the great Rabbi Yehoshua of ancient Israel. While it is true that the giver benefits from having done a Mitzvah and feels good about having done it, the food in a hungry person's body far supercedes those benefits. So, too, having a new roof over one's head after a hurricane has torn the old one apart. In fact, I believe this is a general rule of Tikun Olam: No matter what the benefits to the giver, the recipient's benefit is always more immediate and much more "real".

Will Your Personality Change if You Do More Tzedakah?

רב אמ, לא נתנו מצוות אלא לצרוף בהן את הבריריות

Rav said:
Mitzvahs were given in order to refine human beings.

(Midrash Leviticus Rabba 13:3 (Margoliot Edition))

The Pocket

Will your personality change if you do more Tzedakah?
It might.
It has for many people.
The Talmud records an interesting passage that addresses human personality:

אמר רבי אילעאי: בשלשה דברים אדם ניכר
בכוסו ובכיסו ובכעסו.

Rabbi Ila'i said:
A person's personality may be sensed by three indicators —
The cup [how the person handles alcohol],
The pocket [how the person uses money],
Anger [what kinds of things anger the person].

(Talmud Eruvin 65b)

"The pocket" — Rabbi Ila'i teaches that one sure way to know a person is to observe how a person uses money both for personal needs and for Tzedakah. Many things make you feel good about yourself. But there really is something special about the specific good feeling that you have when you demonstrate how much you care for others. There is something extraordinarily attractive about alleviating another's worries, pain, or despair. What words are there, really, to describe how you feel when you have taken people whose sadness has overwhelmed them and caused them to feel better for a moment, for a day, a week, or permanently?

One Mitzvah and Then Another and Another

Furthermore, Tzedakah has the power to drive you to do even more Tzedakah. It is, in many ways, addictive in a most positive sense. Almost 2,000 years ago, the brilliant Ben Azzai stated it beautifully and succinctly: שמצוה גוררת מצוה— One Mitzvah exerts a pull on another. (Pirkay Avot 4:2) A friend taught me the same principle in more realistic terms. She explained, "Doing Tzedakah is like eating potato chips. Just as you can't eat only one chip, so, too, with acts of Tzedakah. Doing one Mitzvah gives you a craving for the next." Either way, in Real Life, when you pay for home care aides to take care of Elders so that they won't have to go into a nursing home, that very act of Tzedakah may give you a profound sensation of wanting to do more earthshaking miracles. When you use your money to make a fine Passover meal for a new immigrant, buy life-saving medicine for a widow living on a pittance in Moscow, endow a special needs Torah study program in a day school — it becomes difficult to even think you want to slow down or stop. Just consider what it means to pay for birthday parties for kids somewhere who never had one...boys and girls you will never meet because you want them to know that somewhere, someone really cares about them.

At Your Own Pace

Because everyone by nature is different, the power of Tzedakah can influence and shape people at different rates and at different times in their lives. People respond in various ways, and you would do well not to make comparisons with how others may have changed. For some, Tzedakah's intense attraction is like simple addition: one Mitzvah-money-generated deed generates another. Others may move exponentially: Buying three pairs of shoes for people whose own shoes are tattered may lead them to 3^3 —27 more pairs. There are no guarantees, but most likely you will find yourself somewhere within that range.

You may possibly be someone who feels that you have some rough edges that cause irritation, embarrassment, or dismay in others. (I certainly do.) This may make you uncomfortable, and you find yourself living with a poor self-image. Or, you may be troubled that you have acquired a reputation for being condescending or abrasive. Consider one example: arrogance. At first glance, the awesome power of Tzedakah and humility would appear to be a classic contradiction in terms. And yet, since the essence of Tzedakah is both the Life-force and the spiritual affirmation of Life, you might feel humbled by this human gift. In theological terms, you would express gratitude to the Giver of Life for being allowed to spend your days doing Tikun Olam.

Many Ways to Acquire a Sterling Soul

In the world of personality refinement, there are, of course, abundant and diverse methods to repair an injured psyche. Engaging in more Tzedakah is one such method which you may wish to keep in mind. As it has benefited others, it may also work well for you. Possibly, it will even work wonders for your Self. If you do feel a certain disappointment about the way you have treated others (and yourself), doing more Tzedakah can serve as a constant reminder that you are capable of being a deeply caring, even noble, human being. You can assure yourself that ultimately this is the kind of person you are.

To repeat the question: Will my personality change if I do more Tzedakah? Not necessarily and certainly not automatically. But you have changed the odds, and you have changed them far better than you might have expected. Tzedakah does not operate by the same rules as mathematics. Still, even though no precise "ratio of Tzedakah to positive change in personality" exists, you may very well find yourself kinder, more understanding, patient, and gentle than you were before.

Developing a Tzedakah Habit

Rabbi Tanhum, though he needed only one portion of meat for himself, would buy two; one bunch of vegetables, he would buy two—one for the poor and one for himself." (Kohelet Rabba 7:30) Rabbi Tanhum was establishing a regulating pattern in his life, a Tzedakah-habit.

Rabbi Tanhum developed a Tzedakah habit for his life. What are other Tzedakah habits you can think of? How can you pattern them into your own life?

Will You Be a Tzaddik/Tzadeket If You Give Tzedakah?

"I am convinced that the sense of meaning grows not by spectacular acts but by quiet deeds day by day."
Rabbi Abraham Joshua Heschel, ז"ל

Yes...at least at that moment of giving. Unfortunately, the term "צדיק-Tzaddik (m), צדקת-Tzadeket (f)" is too often translated "righteous person". Actually, it frequently means "a good person", "a Mensch." Grammatically, "Tzedakah" and "Tzaddik/Tzadeket" are from the same Hebrew root –צ–ד–ק. The language itself shows that there is an intimate connection between the Tzedakah-act and the person-doing-Tzedakah at any given moment. Still, Tzedakah-deeds are only momentary events in your life, occurring more orless frequently as you establish your own pattern of giving.

One Jewish text elucidates the connection between yourself and what you have accomplished by your deed:

מאי צדיק...בעל צדקות
"What is a 'Tzaddik'? A Tzedakah-oriented person (Ba'al Tzedakot)."
(Kallah Rabbati, Chapter 8)

What Jewish tradition is teaching is that doing the Mitzvah of Tzedakah may, should, or could lead to more than simply a string of giving-moments. Doing Tzedakah can become a regular point of reference and general framework for your way of life. If life's goal, or one of Life's goals, is to become a Tzaddik-צדיק, then certainly giving Tzedakah is one way to achieve that goal...in conjunction. Of course, with a pattern of גמילות חסדים-Gemillut Chassadim, personal acts of caring, lovingkindness.

Understandably, there is a proviso. This text does not mean that a Tzedakah-oriented person who has a mean streak, is overbearing, or mistreats people in other ways can continue to behave in this fashion. Being a lousy human being and a Ba'al Tzedakot-בעל צדקות are a contradiction in terms. In one of his sermons, my teacher, student, and friend, Rabbi Mark Greenspan, explained this entire issue most eloquently:

> Maybe we're a little uncomfortable with this idea, but Judaism teaches us that each of us has the potential to be a Tzaddik...No one has a right to say, 'I'm just an ordinary person trying to make a living.' Each moment has the potential for greatness. We must look for those special moments. Judaism challenges us to strive for righteousness in our lives, not by doing great things, but by doing ordinary things, by living an ordinary life that makes a difference. Winston Churchill once said: "We make a living by what we get. We make a life by what we give."

Rabbi Greenspan is correct on both counts: that anyone can strive to be a Tzaddik, that it is a good and right thing to do, and that this very grand goal can be achieved..."by doing ordinary things, by living an ordinary life that makes a difference."

Benefits of Giving

What Benefits Will You Receive? What Dividends Will Accrue, and What Return Will You Get on Your Investments When You Give Tzedakah?

There is a wonderful story from Talmudic literature that answers this question most eloquently beyond The Big Four, namely: (1) Financially, if you give to a tax-exempt organization, you get a tax deduction; (2) psychologically, you feel good; (3) spiritually, you have a sense of meaning in your life, and (4) physically, you are invigorated.

The story goes as follows:
In the 1st century of the Common Era, there was a Jewish kingdom in a place called Adiabene in what is presently modern-day Iraq. King Munbaz II, son of Queen Helena and Munbaz I, did a most curious thing — he emptied the royal treasury and used the money for the benefit of his subjects who were in need. According to one version (Talmud Bava Batra 11a), a calamitous drought had devastated his kingdom. Another text (Jerusalem Talmud, Pe'ah 1: 1) doesn't record any specific stimulus, which would imply that King Munbaz had reached the stark realization that his subjects normally had enormous pressing needs. Whichever account you study, you can certainly understand that his relatives were not at all pleased with what he did. Here is their exchange with the king:

שלחו לו קרוביו ואמרו לו

אבותיך הוסיפו על שלהן ועל של אבותיהן

ואתה ביזבזתה את שלך ואת של אבותיך

א"ל כל שכן

אבותי גנזו בארץ ואני גנזתי בשמים...

אבותי גנזו אוצרות שאין עושין פירות

ואני גנזתי אוצרות שהן עושין פירות...

אבותי גנזו במקום שהיד שולטת בו

ואני גנזתי במקום שאין היד שולטת בו...

אבותי גנזו ממון ואני גנזתי נפשות...

אבותי גנזו לאחרים ואני גנזתי לעצמי...

אבותי גנזו בעולם הזה ואני גנזתי לעולם הבא...

His relatives sent him a message, saying, "The generation before you accumulated even greater treasures than their ancestors. Now see what you have done! You have wasted both your own wealth and that of your ancestors!"
King Munbaz replied, "I have outdone them all.
"My ancestors accumulated earthly things; I have gathered things for Heaven....
"My ancestors saved money that did not pay dividends; my money is paying dividends....
"My ancestors stored things that could be stolen; mine can't be stolen....
"My ancestors amassed money; I have collected souls....
"My ancestors hoarded things that wound up in the possession of other people; what I have done will always be mine....
"My ancestors held on to things for this world; what I have is being held in The Next World."

In a preceding chapter, I mention that Jewish tradition does not allow for giving away more than 20% of your income except in extreme and clearly-defined circumstances, one of them being that wealthy people may give away more. I suspect that the usual "maximum 20% rule" applies to us "regular people" and that somewhere, somehow, Munbaz had additional funds to provide for his own needs. However you choose to explain that aspect of the tale, Munbaz's answers are eloquent, beautiful, and profound. They express the true benefits and dividends of giving Tzedakah.

Is There a Connection Between Money and Wisdom?

אמר רבי ישמעאל
הרוצה שיחכים יעסוק בדיני ממונות
שאין לך מקצוע בתורה גדול מהן שהן כמעין הנובע
והרוצה שיעסוק בדיני ממונות ישמש את שמעון בן ננס

Rabbi Yishmael said:
Whoever wants to acquire wisdom should study the laws relating to money matters (civil law), because there is no Torah-subject greater than this. This topic is like an ever-flowing stream. And whoever studies the laws of money matters should be an intern with Shimon Ben Nannas.

(Talmud Bava Batra, last Mishnah)

Rabbi Yishmael's teaching seems to mix two realms of human experience — (1) the high and abstract, i.e. wisdom, and (2) mundane situations based on very commonplace experiences. The following comments should help clarify Rabbi Yishmael's words:

Wisdom: Meaning — the power to take accumulated knowledge and experience and grasp certain rules, truths, and principles about the world, Life, and human beings. "Wisdom" means to move beyond the simplistic, such as "All people are basically good." "Wisdom" means that the terrorists who flew their planes into the World Trade Center and Pentagon were evil people. "Wisdom" means to incontrovertibly reject arguments such as, "Well, Hitler kept the trains running on time." Jewish wisdom tells us that we do not achieve wisdom by starting from an intellectual blank page and then building a theory. Rather, wisdom comes by studying significant Jewish texts, assimilating the relevant facts, analyzing experiences, and reflecting on human reactions and interactions in individual real-Life situations. Then, and only then, should you move on to more general principles.

Study the laws relating to money matters: If you want to take basic, earthy examples of human interaction, you won't find a better field of observation than civil and criminal cases involving money. Page after page of the Talmud deals with these issues, and, even though the arguments are often very complicated, you do not have to be an attorney to understand the topics under discussion. Just think for a moment about all the money issues you have encountered in the media: lawsuits both just and frivolous, fights over wills, fraudulent insurance claims, protesting the protesters not wanting a group home for adults with special needs in your neighborhood, fences, fines, alimony and child support issues, personal injury claims, negligence, unfair labor practices, deceptive business practices, returning merchandise, refunds, perjury, loans, scheduling debt repayments, assault and battery, and harassment, all barely touch the range of issues. And one way or another, you know about them.

Ever-flowing stream: The subject matter will nourish and continue to nourish your Jewish soul like water to a thirsty body.

Intern with Shimon ben Nannas: Everyone needs an expert to help him or her work through the complexities of the issues of interpersonal relations. It is more than just clerking with a circuit court judge. Interning with Shimon means not just learning the law and how it works, but also whether or not it is just, and, if not, how the law can be changed. Because he was not only a legal expert, but equally important, steeped in Jewish law and Judaism as a way of life, discussions of priorities would also include justice and mercy in the law, the law as derived from divine sources, rulings based on an awareness that not only human beings are following the flow of history, but also God, Creator of heaven and earth, who freed us from the Land of Egypt, and gave us this freedom to do Tikun Olam. Everyone needs a guide such as Shimon ben Nannas.

That is the intimate relationship between money matters and wisdom.

In Conclusion

**Upon Considering That, In a Few Months,
My Tzedakah Fund Will Have Reached
The $1,000,000 Mark**

Originally printed in *The Meadow Beyond the Meadow: Poems by Danny Siegel, 1991*

I think of those college kids wanting to make
their first million by twenty-five. (I am forty-six
and slower.) It wasn't so long ago,
really, you read about their greed in the polls.

In and of itself, a million is nice to have,
but it was their tone, their playing-field energy for
it, that threw us off.

Well, soon — with God's help — June at the
latest,
I, too, will be a millionaire, thanks to my friends,
their wallets, sixteen years their hands in their
pockets.

How to celebrate it, how mark this event
never again to happen in one life only?

"It" is the million dollars, not mine for keeps,
to be sure. "It" is ten thousand hundreds of them,
given to buy machines that a baby may live
against the unfairest of odds, that a Jew not go
hungry
on Shabbas, that transit to freedom from slurs
and truncheons will be safe, smoother
than my own family's trek from Europe.

In the eighth year, in the tenth, I did not think,
"A half a million!" Halves do not satisfy. Even
at three-quarters there was no projection; a
million was
far too far away, still unthinkable.

But a million....A million the mind can play with —
a million ones scattered in a big room

to jump into the piles like Autumn leaves, or a
thousand
thousand dollar bills (though I have yet to see one
outside of Las Vegas, hold one in my hands),
stacked
ever so neatly in rows on the desk, so much
humble power.

So much Mitzvah in cash, how to arrange the
Simcha?

What will preserve in an hour or two
all those lonelinesses broken by distant givers,
all those steps, now ramps, all the foster parents
loving children, thinking of adoption, all the same
children
waiting to be found?

I will, soon — with God's help — be a millionaire,
and a few of us will gather, sing some Al HaNissim
song
for all the miracles, recite Shehecheyanu,
and drink To Life and perhaps exchange silly
phrases like
"Praise the Lord and pass the pushka" to ease us
into the awe of the occasion.

We will promise to gather again some time hence,
at the end of the next million and the beginning
of yet another. All of that is clear, but much more —
with God's help again — will come of its own.

Whatever the specifics, I know
I shall be the richest millionaire on earth.

Down at the Triple-T Truck Stop

Years ago in one of my books, I re-told a story I had read in the newspaper. It was about a certain Ira Morris, who owned a truck stop in Arizona called the Triple-T. The story interested me for two reasons. First of all, I had once been a truck driver. For 10 months during 1972-1973 I drove The Atid-United Synagogue Bookmobile around the country. It was a 29' vehicle filled with Jewish books that were sold at - as best as I recall - 134 stops I made along the way. So, I had been in a few truck stops in my day, even though compared to the humongous semis parked to the right and the left of the bookmobile, mine seemed a little bit like a toy. Still, miniature truck or not, I was a trucker and my Mom and Dad were proud that they had raised a kid who had gotten two bachelor's degrees in four-and-a-half years of college and then a master's in another couple of years…seven years post-high school in all. They felt good that all that 20th century comparative literature, Bible, and Talmud would serve me well riding high on the interstates.

The second reason had more to do with what made the Triple-T different than other truck stops. Mr. Morris had added two elements no one else had thought of - a rocking chair and a very friendly cat. Both were available to any trucker who might need a special break beyond a standard long-haul driver's meal and cup of coffee before heading down the road again. They could pick up the kitty, sit in the rocking chair, and relax for as long as they wanted. Clearly, everyone was happy: the trucker, the owner, and, without a doubt, the cat.

Now, years after reading that story, my mind is wandering and I am beginning to wonder -
Is it possible that a truck driver climbed into the cab less stressed out than he would have been without the break in the rocking chair with the cat on his lap? It's possible.

Did he drive just a few miles per hour slower, closer to the speed limit, and 20% more carefully because he felt good? Perhaps.

Did the driver stay 27% more awake because - aside the coffee - he was in a good mood? Maybe. Because the driver was feeling good and that much more awake on the long haul, is it possible that this one driver avoided some obstacle in the road, prevented a jackknife, a pile-up, his dying in a twisted wreck, and the deaths of other drivers and passengers? It is entirely possible that all of that didn't happen.

When the driver got home, did he or she hug and kiss his or her spouse and children differently?

Maybe.

Did all of this happen and not happen to this driver? There's really no way to know for certain, but it is possible.

To two drivers? Possibly.

To 10, 20, 50, 100 during the lifetime of a cat? Quite possibly.

How many more heartbeats were added to the world's total? Billions upon billions.

Grand total, how much did the rocking chair and 14 years of cat food cost?

You save one life, you save the world.

Joe the Butler

Years ago in another one of my books, I re-told a story I had read in the newspaper. It was about a certain Joe Lejman who used to dress up as a butler and serve in a local shelter for victims of domestic violence. I thought it was a brilliant idea. The article I had read was a short blurb, so there was only one incident-moment that the reporter chose to relate. I had hoped for more, but, in retrospect, and with years to reflect, I understand the reporter's wisdom. The incident was The Incident, the one that would teach us almost everything we needed to know about Joe Lejman and his marvelous Mitzvah.

As it happened, one day, Joe had finished serving a meal for the residents, then poured the coffee. He poured for one woman, and then lit her cigarette. She began to cry. She cried because she told Joe that this was the first time she could remember that anyone had done something nice for her.

Now, years after reading that story, my mind is wandering and I am beginning to wonder -
Is it possible that this woman regained every shred of her lost self-respect because of Joe Lejman's single act of unadulterated caring and radiant goodness? It's possible.

Did she then tell the social workers she had emerged from her despair, regained her energy, and wanted to go job hunting the next day? She might have.

Did she then get a job, give the appropriate portion of her first and every subsequent paycheck to Tzedakah, do homework with her kids at night, and help get them through high school and into college? Perhaps.

Did the children then go to college, graduate, get jobs, give the appropriate percentage of their first and every subsequent paycheck to Tzedakah, and raise their families to do the same? Maybe they did.
Were the other women in that shelter so inspired by what she did that they did the same, start life all over again because of Joe Lejman? Maybe they did, too.

How many more heartbeats were added to the world's total? Billions upon billions.

How far out into the entire population of Planet Earth did the concentric circles reach because Joe Lejman, one man, got this crazy idea to be a butler in a shelter for women, who, by all reasonable possibility, should have sunk into lifelong oblivion?

Grand total, how much did Joe spend on a butler's outfit?

You save one life, you save the world.

תִּקוּן עוֹלָם

UNITED SYNAGOGUE YOUTH
TIKUN OLAM POLICY

WHAT IS TIKUN OLAM? Tikun Olam is the vehicle through which money is contributed to Tzedakah by United Synagogue Youth. We recognize the value of the individual of giving Tzedakah, and we realize the importance of helping others. One major way that this is done in the world today is through financial assistance.

WHO BENEFITS? The limited financial resources of Tikun Olam, "Building a Better World," allow that only Jewish causes be included on the approved list of Tzedakot. If a chapter wishes to allocate funds to a local non-Jewish Tzedakah, it must write the Central Office for approval. The list of approved Tzedakot includes hospitals, orphanages, and social service organizations, and also Tzedakot that provide for the development of individual Jewish communities worldwide. Tikun Olam also benefits the growth and success of the Conservative Movement in North America and Israel, through the support of the Jewish Theological Seminary and Noam Masorti, our sister organization in Israel.

"ALL ISRAEL IS RESPONSIBLE FOR ONE ANOTHER": If we do not help the Jewish world, who will? And by helping our fellow Jews, we increase Jewish potential for helping others.

SUPPORT FOR PROGRAMS IN ISRAEL AND SCHOLARSHIP ASSISTANCE: Our commitment to Conservative Movement's programs in Israel and USY summer and long-term programs is obvious and essential because they serve each chapter and region directly. The programs in Israel provide many of the future teachers and rabbis to guide our communities. Scholarships to USYers participating on USY summer and long term programs are beneficial because of the special spirit and enthusiasm that develop during these trips. One look into the eyes of a recent summer program participant will convince anyone of the importance of these programs. For these reasons, Tikun Olam is structured to provide 30% of its funds to the Conservative Movement Programs in Israel (as well as covering the operating expenses of the program and educational materials about Tzedakah) while another 30% is returned to regions to provide scholarships for USYers participating in summer and long-term programs.

USYERS RAISE AND ALLOCATE ALL FUNDS: Basic to the Jewish concept of Tzedakah is the direct participation of every individual. Therefore, our chapters and regions do not contribute what is "left over" in their treasury for Tikun Olam; instead they plan specific events and drives in which their members actively raise money. Therefore, each chapter and region individually decides which Tzedakot the remaining 40% of this contribution will assist.

TIKUN OLAM IS THE EXCLUSIVE TZEDAKAH FUND FOR USY: In order to assist the Tzedakot that we support, Tikun Olam collects its funds centrally. By donating our contribution in one lump sum, we allow our Tzedakot to plan special programs meeting their major needs, whereas small contributions only allow these charities to pay for operating expenses. Most importantly, since the Tikun Olam program was created and is run by USYers, all Tzedakah is contributed through Tikun Olam.

Appendix B
How to Read the IRS Form 990 and Find Out What it Means

On the next few pages, we will take a look at an IRS Form 990 and see what information we can find on it that is helpful for our Tzedakah research. Begin by looking at particular items and examine them carefully. The following is in no way definitive, but should serve as a guide and point of departure for your research:

1. What is the organization's total revenue?
2. What is the source/are the sources of the organization's revenue?
3. How much was spent on
   A. Program?
   B. Management?
   C. Fundraising?
4. What are the organization's net assets?
5. How many people are on the organization's staff, and how much is their compensation?
6. The board:
   A. How many people sit on the organization's board?
   B. Who are they?
   C. Are they compensated in any way for serving on the board?
7. How much does the organization spend on travel and entertainment?

Again, these questions are merely a point of departure for your thorough investigation.

Form 990 is an annual reporting return that certain federally tax-exempt organizations must file with the IRS. It provides information on the filing organization's mission, programs, and finances. Before you choose to donate to any Tzedakah, you should look for a copy of its IRS Form 990 (using a website like Guidestar.org) to determine what the organization does with the money.

#1-Identity and Tax Status—At the top of page 1 of the Form 990 there is a section of about seven lines that asks for the name of the filing organization and certain other information. On this page, you will want to make sure that it was filed in the current fiscal year, that it is the final return for that year, and that you are looking at the correct organization–and not one with a simlar name.

#2 -How Much Income Did the Filer Receive and From What Sources?—This page will start to give you an idea of how much income the organization has, where they spend their money, and what the likelihood is that the organization will be able to function with or without your support.

Part I	Revenue, Expenses, and Changes in Net Assets or Fund Balances (See Specific Instructions on page 16.)			
1	Contributions, gifts, grants, and similar amounts received:			
a	Direct public support	1a	1,500,000	
b	Indirect public support	1b		
c	Government contributions (grants)	1c		
d	Total (add lines 1a through 1c) (cash $ 1,500,000 noncash $ _____)	1d		1,500,000
2	Program service revenue including government fees and contracts (from Part VII, line 93)	2		
3	Membership dues and assessments	3		
4	Interest on savings and temporary cash investments	4		55,000
5	Dividends and interest from securities	5		105,000
6a	Gross rents	6a		
b	Less: rental expenses	6b		
c	Net rental income or (loss) (subtract line 6b from line 6a)	6c		
7	Other investment income (describe ▶)	7		
8a	Gross amount from sales of assets other than inventory	(A) Securities 8a	(B) Other	
b	Less: cost or other basis and sales expenses	8b		
c	Gain or (loss) (attach schedule)	8c		
d	Net gain or (loss) (combine line 8c, columns (A) and (B))	8d		
9	Special events and activities (attach schedule)			
a	Gross revenue (not including $ _____ of contributions reported on line 1a)	9a		
b	Less: direct expenses other than fundraising expenses	9b		
c	Net income or (loss) from special events (subtract line 9b from line 9a)	9c		
10a	Gross sales of inventory, less returns and allowances	10a		
b	Less: cost of goods sold	10b		
c	Gross profit or (loss) from sales of inventory (attach schedule) (subtract line 10b from line 10a)	10c		
11	Other revenue (from Part VII, line 103)	11		
12	Total revenue (add lines 1d, 2, 3, 4, 5, 6c, 7, 8d, 9c, 10c, and 11)	12		1,660,000
13	Program services (from line 44, column (B))	13		962,000
14	Management and general (from line 44, column (C))	14		222,000
15	Fundraising (from line 44, column (D))	15		296,000
16	Payments to affiliates (attach schedule)	16		
17	Total expenses (add lines 16 and 44, column (A))	17		1,480,000
18	Excess or (deficit) for the year (subtract line 17 from line 12)	18		180,000
19	Net assets or fund balances at beginning of year (from line 73, column (A))	19		1,500,000
20	Other changes in net assets or fund balances (attach explanation)	20		
21	Net assets or fund balances at end of year (combine lines 18, 19, and 20)	21		1,680,000

For Paperwork Reduction Act Notice, see page 1 of the separate Instructions.　　Cat. No. 11282Y　　Form 990 (2000)

#3-How Did the Filer's Total Expenses Break Down Among Program, Management, and Fundraising Expenses?—Program expenses are those incurred to help the organization carry out its mission. By simply dividing a particular functional expense total by total expenses, one can learn what percent of total expenses have been spent on that function. For example, in the example from a Form 990 set out below, program expenses make up 60% of total expenses ($1,200,000/$2,000,000 = 60%).

13	Program services (from line 44, column (B))	13	1,200,000
14	Management and general (from line 44, column (C))	14	200,000
15	Fundraising (from line 44, column (D))	15	600,000
16	Payments to affiliates (attach schedule)	16	
17	Total expenses (add lines 16 and 44, column (A))	17	2,000,000

Other questions to ask of information included on the 990 Form include:

#4-What Can You Tell From Net Assets?—This information will indicate whether the filer operated at a surplus or deficit for the year being reported on and the size of such surplus or deficit. This is of obvious interest since on the face of it a surplus and its size may suggest future financial health while a deficit and its size may suggest future financial difficulty. If you have access to three or more years of the filer's Forms 990 and they indicate a trend of surpluses or deficits, this may be more significant as a predictor of the filer's future financial condition.

#5 What Kinds of Programs Does the Filer Run and How Much Does It Spend on Them? The filer is required to state the organization's primary purpose on a very short line near the top of this part. Then for each program it conducts the filer is to describe, on several lines provided for this, each such program's purpose, stating the outputs of the program, such as number of clients served, publications issued, and students taught. In a column to the right of this description, the filer is to list the total of program expenses for each such program.

#6 Who are the Filer's Board Members and How Much Does its Top Staff Get Paid? The name of each board member is listed. (The address of each board member is also given, but in many cases the address will be the same as the address of the filer). If the board member receives any compensation for her or his duties, the amounts are reported here. Of course, most board members do not receive compensation for their work as board members.

#7 Did the Filer Initiate Some New Activity, Change Its Processes for Governing or Engage in Any Excess Benefit Transactions? If there is any changes in activity or by-laws that could change the organization's exempt status, it must disclose that and include details of those changes.

#8 Did the Filer Engage in any Self-DealingTransactions During the Year? An example of such a transaction might be the sale by a board member of property he owns to the nonprofit organization on whose board he sits at a price in excess of its fair market value.

#9 Is the Filer a Private Foundation? All section 501(c)(3) nonprofits are either private foundations or non-private foundations. The term "private foundation" is a technical term and relates to the kind of nonprofit an organization is and the nature of its support and not to the fact it is a philanthropy. (We will refer to a non-private foundation as a "public charity.") This distinction between private foundation and public charity is important since, from a nonprofit's standpoint, it is undesirable to be a private foundation. For example, there are some significant limits on making contributions to private foundations, and private foundations are generally prohibited from doing any lobbying and must pay a small excise tax.

#10 Does the Filer Lobby? A number of nonprofit groups advocate for changes in public policy and as part of their advocacy efforts engage in lobbying. The term "lobbying" refers to attempts to influence legislators (or those who work with them) to support or oppose the enactment of some legislation. It may be done by directly contacting legislators (direct lobbying) or by asking others to contact them (grass roots lobbying). Organizations exempt under section 501(c)(3) are permitted to engage in some lobbying, but if they do too much they may jeopardize their tax-exemption.

For more information about interpreting the IRS 990 Form, please visit Nonprofit Coordinating Committee of New York, Inc at www.npccny.org.

About the Author

Danny Siegel, officially founded the Ziv Tzedakah Fund in 1981 after making several trips to Israel. Our tradition teaches that anyone on a Mitzvah mission will be saved from harm, and so, on each trip, Danny followed this age-old custom and asked friends and relatives for a dollar or two to give away to Tzedakah upon his arrival in the Holy Land. Once in Israel, Danny went in search of "the Good People", ordinary Israelis who were working tirelessly and simply trying to make the world a better place.

In the 1970s, in Israel, within a short time, he learned of the efforts of such greats as Hadassah Levi, who made her life's work the rescue of abandoned Down Syndrome babies from hospitals, Myriam Mendilow, who found Jerusalem's poor, elderly residents on the streets of the city and gave them respect and new purpose in her program, Yad L'Kashish (Lifeline for the Old), and Uri Lupolianski, a young teacher who started Israel's now famous medical equipment lending program, Yad Sarah, in his living room (and is now the current mayor of Jerusalem). (While Ziv supported Lifeline and Yad Sarah for many years, they have grown and are very self-sufficient now!)

Returning from each trip, Danny wrote a one-page report to all of his donors in which he described all of the places that he had distributed their Tzedakah money. From that first $955 Danny collected and gave away, Ziv has grown to an organization that in 2004 completed its 29th year of operation and has distributed more than $6,700,000.

Danny is a well-known author, lecturer, and poet who has spoken in more than 500 North American Jewish communities, to synagogues, JCC's, Federations, and other communal organizations on Tzedakah and Jewish values, besides reading from his own poetry. He is the author of 29 books on such topics as Mitzvah heroes and practical and personalized Tzedakah, and has produced an anthology of 500 selections of Talmudic quotes about living the Jewish life well called Where Heaven and Earth Touch. Danny is also a poet and several of his published books are poetry.

Danny has been referred to as "The World's Greatest Expert on Microphilanthropy", "The Feeling Person's Thinker", and "The Pied Piper of Tzedakah".

Danny has a B.S. in Comparative Literature from Columbia University's School of General Studies, and a Bachelor's and Master's of Hebrew Literature from the Jewish Theological Seminary of America.

He is one of three recipients of the prestigious 1993 Covenant Award for Exceptional Jewish Educators. Danny has been a scholar-in-residence for the USY Israel Pilgrimage program for over 30 years and served as USY International President in 1962.